AQUARIUM FISHES
in color

AQUARIUM FISHES
in color

Jens M. Madsen

Color illustrations by
Kjeld Warthoe Sorensen

MACMILLAN PUBLISHING CO., INC.
New York

English text © 1975 Blandford Press Ltd
World Copyright © 1974
Politikens Forlag A/S Copenhagen

MACMILLAN PUBLISHING CO., INC.
866 Third Avenue, New York, N.Y. 10022

Library of Congress Cataloging in Publication Data

Madsen, Jens.
    Aquarium fishes in color.

    Bibliography: p.
    Includes indexes.
    1. Aquarium fishes-- Pictorial works.   I.   Title.
SF457.M5   1975   639'.34   74–31451
ISBN 0-02-579170-2

First American Edition 1975

Color section printed in Denmark
Text printed in Great Britain

CONTENTS

FOREWORD

This edition of *Aquarium Fishes in Color* is a completely new book, designed to replace the earlier edition which was published some seventeen years ago.

This book has been designed primarily as an identification handbook for those interested in aquaria. It describes about 450 different species of aquarium fishes from fresh and sea water, and therefore gives an extremely representative selection of those species that are available on the market and can be kept in the home aquarium.

The fishes shown on the colour plates have mostly been drawn from living specimens and with a few exceptions in their natural size. In cases where it is necessary for purposes of identification the plates show not only both sexes, but also changes in coloration, as for example during breeding, and also the appearance of the young stages when this differs from the adult.

The book starts with a short introduction on aquarium maintenance. This is followed by the colour plates and the descriptions of the fishes. In both the plates and the descriptions the fishes are arranged by families. Under each family heading there is a series of characters common to all or nearly all the genera and species in that family. The descriptions of the species themselves are mainly set out on the same plan, to include the scientific or Latin name, the English name, the general appearance and total length, the distribution, habits, breeding and so on. From this it should be easy for the reader either to identify an unknown fish or to seek information on any special conditions of maintenance. Where there is a variance in American and British classification or nomenclature both alternatives are given. The American name appears first and the British name is given directly below it in square brackets. A comprehensive index adds to the value of the book as a reference source.

The selection of species and the text have been carried out by Jens M. Madsen, and the colour illustrations prepared by the artist Kjeld Warthoe Sorensen. The cover design is by Verner Hancke and the distribution maps have been prepared by Arne Gaarn Bak.

The book can be used internationally and there are, or will be editions for Denmark, Finland, France, Holland, Norway, Sweden and Germany, in addition to Britain and the United States.

Editor

INTRODUCTION

AQUARIUM MAINTENANCE

Types of aquarium

The commonest type of aquarium is a tank with a frame of iron, stainless steel or aluminium, the glass slides being held in position by mastic. It is also possible to construct all-glass tanks up to 600–700 litres (158–259·8 U.S. gals), using silicone glue. This has the advantage that one can make tanks of a shape and size to suit one's own requirements. If this is done, the thickness of the glass relative to the volume and height must not be underestimated. The following thicknesses are recommended: up to 15 litres (4 U.S. gals), 3 mm ($\frac{1}{8}$ in.); up to 40 litres (10$\frac{1}{2}$ U.S. gals), 4 mm ($\frac{1}{6}$ in.); up to 70 litres (18$\frac{1}{2}$ U.S. gals), 5–6 mm ($\frac{1}{4}$ in.); up to 100 litres (26$\frac{1}{2}$ U.S. gals), 6–7 mm ($\frac{5}{16}$ in.); up to 350 litres (92$\frac{1}{2}$ U.S. gals), 10 mm ($\frac{3}{8}$ in.). These figures apply to tanks that are not abnormally tall. After thorough removal of grease and oil from the corners and bottom plate, old leaking tanks can be made watertight with silicone glue without the necessity for renewal of all the mastic.

Quite apart from the type chosen, an aquarium tank should always be as large as conditions permit and the surface area should be as large as possible relative to the volume in order to facilitate gaseous exhange at the surface.

The tank should always be placed on a completely flat surface to avoid setting up dangerous stresses in the bottom plate and in the glass side panels. The actual position of the aquarium in the room can be left to personal taste, as the tank is best illuminated by fluorescent strip lights.

Moulded all-glass tanks are only useful for purposes of quarantine and treatment, as the sides are not usually flat. Plastic tanks have the disadvantage that they are easily scratched, and tanks made of asbestos cement with a single viewing window are too clumsy in comparison with angle-iron or silicone-cemented tanks. See also the section on sea-water tanks on page 214.

Setting up the tank

It is impossible to give directions on the most attractive way of setting up an aquarium tank. It is, however, important that one should not use any decorative materials, plants and so on that might have an adverse biological influence or that would not go well with the fish chosen for the tank. The necessary conditions for the well-being of the fish are given under each genus or species, and attention is also drawn to the section on the sea-water aquarium (page 214). Here, however, are a few guide lines.

The substrate
This should normally consist of coarse sand or fine gravel of a mineral which should have the least influence on the water, and be free of metals and calcium salts. Granite, silica sand, feldspar and similar substances are excellent, provided the edges are not too sharp. The substrate should be 25 mm (up to 1 in.) deep so that it is possible to grow some plants. It is an advantage to let it slope down to a special low-lying area, so that detritus and other impurities that collect there can be easily siphoned off. For small, peaceful rain-forest fishes the substrate can be of sphagnum moss, which is very suitable for plant roots, and influences the water in a way beneficial to such species (lower pH, bactericidal action, provision of pro-vitamins).

Decorative materials
In the freshwater aquarium suitable decorative materials include well-washed tree roots, fossil wood, flat natural rocks, and cement structures (the latter are only to be used after a hardening period of two months). In aquarium tanks with hard-water fishes, e.g. Malawi and Tanganyika cichlids, it is an advantage to use limestone or other calcareous materials, as these prevent the pH of the water from falling too low.

Plants
For most aquarists plants are the most important decorative features in freshwater tanks. Apart from their decorative function, plants also give off oxygen when illuminated, and they take in nitrogenous substances (nitrates, etc.) produced by the breakdown of excess food and of the fish excretions. From the purely functional viewpoint, rapid-growing, pale green plants are probably the best producers of oxygen and users of nitrate, but nowadays there is a wealth of aquatic plants to choose from. The arrangement of the plants in the tank is a matter of personal taste.

Technical equipment
Certain technical aids are necessary in order to maintain constant conditions in the aquarium. The principal items are heaters, air and water pumps, filters, lighting, nets and thermometers.

Heaters
Room temperatures are usually some degrees below the temperature at which most aquarium fishes live in the wild, so the tank has to be heated

artificially. This is best done with glass immersion heaters, which can be bought at pet stores. It is advisable to choose a heater with a wattage a little above what is needed, and to connect it to a thermostat set for temperatures of 24–30°C (75–86°F), depending on the requirements of the different fish species. The heater can hang free in a corner of the tank or it can lie *on the surface* of the substrate, but never buried in it.

Air and water pumps

The tank water can be aerated by means of an air pump or kept in circulation by a water pump. The purposes of these operations are to ensure a uniform distribution of temperature in the tank, to increase the uptake of oxygen at the water surface and to provide currents in the water which most fishes like.

The air from the air pump, usually a membrane pump, is led down into the water by a plastic tube and is released through a porous diffuser stone. The stream of fine air bubbles sets the water and the surface in motion.

A circulation pump, powered by a small electric motor, sucks water from one part of the tank and returns it to another. A filter incorporated into this circulatory system can be packed with a filtration medium such as nylon wool, gravel, sphagnum or other material; it will remove many of the impurities from the water, and according to the type of material used may also help to keep the water in good condition.

Filters

Apart from the use of aeration and water circulation the water can also be moved with the help of various forms of internal and external filters, through which the water is driven by air from an air pump. An external filter consists of a watertight container subdivided into two compartments. The first and larger is the filter chamber which is connected with the aquarium tank by a curved or U-shaped tube. The water passes from the tank to the filter chamber, through the filtration medium and then into the second compartment. The clear, filtered water is then lifted from this compartment by a stream of air bubbles (air-lift principle) into a tube which carries it back into the fish tank.

Internal filters of various kinds have been designed, but the only important one is what is known as a bottom filter (subsand or under-gravel filter). This consists of a perforated plastic plate which is raised above the bottom of the tank, so that there is a water chamber below the substrate. A vertical tube is fitted at one corner of the plastic plate, and air is led to its lower end by means of a second narrower tube. This air stream, acting again as an air-lift, sucks water from below the perforated plastic plate and returns it to the top of the tank. The water thus removed from the bottom chamber is replaced by water which has passed through the substrate. By this means the substrate functions as a filter medium.

11

This method can be modified in various ways. The perforated plate can, for example, be replaced by a system of perforated tubes lying beneath the substrate. The advantage of using the substrate as a filter is that it encourages beneficial bacteria that require oxygen and discourages dangerous putrefying bacteria. See also section of sea-water tanks, page 214.

Lighting and other accessories

The cheapest and most effective method of lighting an aquarium tank is to use fluorescent tubes, which are switched on for twelve out of the twenty-four hours. These lights should be fitted in protected shades above the tank's cover glass. For an aquarium with plants the American Sylvania Gro-Lux (TM) or the British Osram 32 de luxe and Philips No. 29 are excellent. Apart from encouraging plant growth they also provide an attractive light in the aquarium. In general, it is best to light the whole length of the tank, using one fluorescent tube for every 20 cm (8 in.) of tank width (the distance between the front and back panes). See also the sea-water section, page 214.

Finally, there are various accessories which are neccessary for the day-to-day care of the fish. These are: reliable thermometers, a couple of coarse-mesh nets for catching fish, a fine-mesh net for the fry and for finely divided food, scrapers to remove algae from the glass, a length of tubing for siphoning water out of the tank and various sieves for sorting out food.

The water

In many localities the mains water has a high content of dissolved calcium and magnesium salts, and such water is said to be hard. On the other hand, most aquarium fishes live in nature in soft water, poor in calcium. In spite of this the majority of these fishes do remarkably well in hard mains water and the same applies to the plants. The only exceptions to the use of hard water would be when rearing young fish, when acclimatising wild-caught rain-forest fishes and when keeping certain 'difficult' fishes such as discus and Chocolate Gourami. The content of calcium salts in the water is expressed in German degrees of hardness (°DH), and 1° DH corresponds to a value of 10 mg calcium, as calcium oxide, per litre (per 1·75 pints) of water. In nature, rain-forest fishes live in water with a hardness less than 1° DH, and for comparison the mains water in many localities may have a hardness in the range 18–20° DH. Young fish should be reared in a soft water, which may be rain water (although in cities rain water is apt to be dangerously contaminated with dissolved 'smog'), distilled water that has been filtered through sphagnum moss, or demineralised water, from which the salts have been removed by an ion exchange resin.

There are special, relatively inexpensive kits on the market which enable the aquarist to measure the hardness of his water, without having to be a skilled chemist.

Another basic factor is the acidity or alkalinity of the water, which is expressed as the pH. When the pH value is below seven, one speaks of acid water, whereas with a pH of above seven the water is alkaline or basic. Water at pH 7·0 is neutral. Within a certain margin of error it is possible to measure the pH with special indicator papers, which are calibrated to show pH values within a certain range. A better but more time-consuming method involves measuring the pH with indicator solutions, and the most accurate but most expensive method is to measure the pH with an electric pH meter. Where the pH value is important it is given under the individual fishes; see also the sea-water section, page 214.

In recent years it has become common practice to change a large or small proportion of the water, for example, one-third every month, in order to remove injurious waste products. Within the scope of this book it would not be possible to discuss all the factors involved in maintaining the water in a condition suitable for fish, and the reader is referred to the bibliography at the end of the book.

Information on other points, such as general husbandry, behaviour, reproduction and so on is given under the individual species or their genera.

FISH ANATOMY AND FUNCTION

The form, coloration and biological characters of a fish species reflect the numerous influences which are continually acting on it. Inherited characters that are unfavourable to the survival of the species will tend to disappear, while those which favour its continued existence in a given environment will be preserved.

Body form
Water offers a large variety of living habitats and this has provided fishes with all sorts of possibilities for specialisation. This is reflected particularly in the shape of the body, for by no means all fishes have the streamlined or torpedo-shaped body characteristic of those that swim fast or live in rivers. With a little practice one can deduce a fish's habits or preferred habitat from the shape of its body and fins. Bottom-living fishes are usually flat or they lie on one side (flatfishes) or they may be eel- or worm-shaped. Fishes that live in the middle water layers, if they need to swim fast or against a strong current, are usually torpedo-shaped with small fins. Tall, laterally compressed fishes, such as discus and angelfish, live in

13

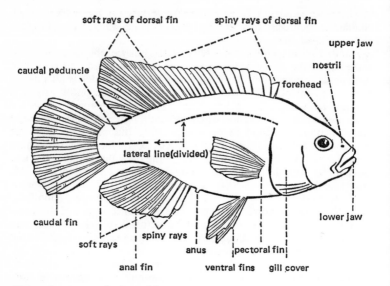

soft rays of dorsal fin | spiny rays of dorsal fin

upper jaw

nostril

caudal peduncle

forehead

lateral line (divided)

caudal fin

soft rays | spiny rays

anus | pectoral fin

anal fin | ventral fins | gill cover

lower jaw

External anatomy of a bony fish.

the vicinity of vegetation or in among the tree roots along the banks of rivers and lakes. Similar forms in sea water, such as Pennant Coralfish (*Heniochus*), Moorish Idol (*Zanclus*) and Batfish (*Platax*) are found near or in among growths of coral. Territorial fishes like the cichlids and many coral reef fishes are usually rather squat with a large head in relation to the body. Surface-living species have a typical straight back, often with a very convex belly; e.g. hatchetfishes. There are numerous variations from these basic types, as for instance, sea-horses, pufferfishes and boxfishes.

Fins
The limbs of fishes, known as fins, consist of thin integument stretched over a skeleton of fin rays which may be either hard, spiny rays (often developed at the front of the dorsal or anal fin) or soft rays. The fin rays are connected to the body by joints and muscles, which enable the fish to move its fins independently of one another. In addition to moving and steering the body the fins have many other behavioural functions, e.g. in fighting, mating and brood protection. The fins are of two types: unpaired, like the dorsal, caudal and anal fins and in some families the little rayless adipose fin, and paired as the pectoral and ventral fins. Certain species swim mainly or entirely by the movements of the fins.

14

Thus, sea-horses and pufferfishes propel themselves by the rapid and undulatory movements of the dorsal and anal fins. Gobies and some wrasses paddle forwards with the pectoral fins. Knifefishes swim by the undulations of the long anal fin. In the mudskippers the ventral fins serve as supports, functioning almost as feet. In many fishes the fins also carry various sense organs.

Skin and scales

The outer surface of a fish's body is covered with skin, consisting of an outer thin epidermis and deeper tough dermis in which the scales are embedded. The epidermis is coated with a thin layer of mucus, which forms a valuable protection against infections and reduces friction between the body and the water during swimming.

In almost all aquarium fishes the body is covered with scales. In bony fishes these are thin bony plates arranged from head to tail like tiles on a roof. The scales vary considerably in size. In the Mahseer, a large game-fish from India, the scales are the size of a man's hand. Eels have micro-scopic scales. In boxfishes the scales are fused to form a hard, box-like external 'skeleton'. The scales of sea-horses are modified as rings of fused bony plates. The commonest types of scale are the ctenoid with a toothed rear edge and the cycloid with a rounded rear edge. The scales grow with the fish, and as the growth of a fish depends on a varying food supply, the scales reflect these conditions just like the annual rings in a tree trunk, and so they can be used in determining the age of an individual fish. In the case of aquarium fishes this applies only to cold-water species or to species that live under varying conditions.

Many fish species, such as catfishes, loaches and barbs, have barbels round the mouth, which carry taste buds that help the fish to orientate itself. Other skin appendages on the head and body may serve as camouflage or as secondary sexual characters.

Colours

The colours may be due to physical factors, involving the reflection or interference of the light striking the body, or they may be due to the presence of chemical pigments in special cells of the dermis. In nature the colours of a fish have two opposing functions. One is passive, namely to camouflage the individual so that it is less visible to its natural enemies or to its prey. The other is active, to ensure that the fish is seen, either to warn off predators and rivals or to attract a mate and members of its own shoal.

Let us give a couple of examples of camouflage. One of the basic principles is the so-called countershading. Thus, the back of a fish is darker than the belly. If one imagines a fish that is equally pale or dark on its back and belly the effect of light from above would be to make it more

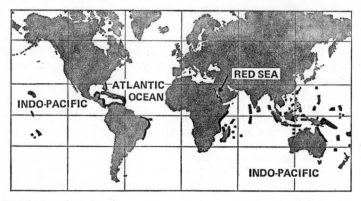

Distribution of coral reefs

conspicuous. On the other hand, countershading helps to blur the fish's contours. This principle is well shown in the Upside-down Catfish, *Synodontis nigriventris*, which normally swims back-downwards and has a dark belly. In many popular aquarium fishes countershading is reinforced by disruptive patterns. This can be seen in the vertical dark and pale stripes of the Tiger Barb. At a quick glance the dark stripes appear to be farther away than the pale ones, so that the body of the fish is optically disrupted. The same applies to spotted patterns.

In many cases the eyes of a fish are so well camouflaged as to be almost invisible. Often a vertical or horizontal stripe runs right though the eye.

Skeleton

The specialisation of fishes for swimming is reflected in the skeleton and musculature. The internal skeleton of a bony fish consists of a number of bones which support and provide attachments for the muscles.

This skeleton consists of the cranium, vertebral column, shoulder and pelvic girdles and the ribs. The numerous bones in the cranium provide protection for the brain as well as its associated sense organs. The jaws are attached to the cranium. The gill arches support the gills which are covered by gill covers consisting of a number of flat bones.

In many fishes there are characteristic small bones between the muscles (intermuscular bones).

Muscles

The skeletal muscles of a fish enable it to swim. They are arranged in segments or myomeres. These can be best seen after the skin has been removed. The individual myomeres are attached to the intervening

16

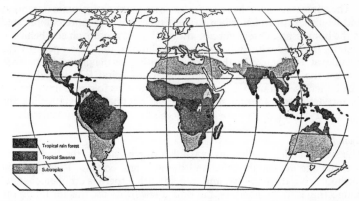

The geographical distribution of tropical rain-forest and tropical savanna, the two principal biotopes for freshwater aquarium fishes, showing their boundaries with subtropical areas.

connective tissue membranes, supported by the intermuscular bones. This is in contrast to the muscles of land animals which are attached directly to the bones. The musculature of the body is characterised by an upper and lower band of powerful muscles which are particularly important for the body's movement and which are attached behind to the base of the caudal fin.

Both the unpaired and the paired fins have numerous muscles which individually or in groups are capable of raising and lowering the fin rays. In most fishes the body musculature is used in swimming, although a few use the fins. Pufferfishes and pipefishes move by the vibrations of the dorsal fin, knifefishes and others swim by the undulatory movements of the anal fin; by reversing these undulations a knifefish can swim backwards. Other fishes paddle themselves forwards with the pectoral fins, e.g. gobies.

Digestive system

Bony fishes have a mouth at the front end of the body, which is turned downwards in bottom-living species (e.g. catfishes, loaches), upwards in surface-living fishes (e.g. hatchetfishes, archerfishes), or forwards in fishes from the middle water layers (e.g. perch and similar fishes). The teeth are very variable in form and arrangement. Some species have teeth only along the edges of the jaws, others also have teeth on the roof of the mouth and in the pharynx. Some have long, pointed teeth adapted for seizing prey, others have flat, crushing teeth. On each side of the pharynx there are openings which lead to the gills.

17

The alimentary canal has its simplest form in the cyclostomes (lampreys and hagfishes) in which it is a straight tube, but it is more complicated in the bony fishes. Often, but not always there is a stomach and behind it a short intestine with only a few convolutions, and this opens to the outside at the anus. In the more primitive cartilaginous fishes (e.g. sharks) the inner side of the intestine has a spiral fold (spiral valve) which increases its surface area. In bony fishes this fold is reduced or has disappeared, and a larger surface area is obtained by lengthening the alimentary canal, or in some cases by the development of diverticula.

Swimbladder

The swimbladder is a hollow, gas-filled organ lying in the body cavity between the alimentary canal and the vertebral column. It arises as an offshoot from the pharynx, and in many fishes there is an open channel connecting it to the pharynx, but only a few fishes use this for filling the swimbladder. In certain primitive fishes, such as garpike (*Lepisosteus*) the swimbladder is used as a respiratory organ, but in most it functions as a hydrostatic organ. By altering the volume of its swimbladder a fish can regulate its specific gravity so that this comes as close as possible to that of the surrounding water, and this helps the fish to maintain buoyancy. The use by certain primitive fishes of the swimbladder as a respiratory organ supports the idea that this was its original function and that the hydrostatic function is secondary.

Gills

The gills are built on the same basic pattern in both the cartilaginous and the bony fishes. In cartilaginous fishes each side of the pharynx has a series of openings, usually five, into the gill chambers which contain the gills. The gill chambers open to the outside via the gill slits, which in sharks appear as a row of vertical slits one behind the other on the sides of the head. The gill chambers are separated from one another by the gill arches. The gills themselves are attached to the gill arches and consist of a series of very much folded pockets covered with a thin layer of cells that is permeable to gases in solution and contains a well-developed system of blood capillaries.

In addition to functioning as respiratory organs the gills serve a number of other roles. The gill surfaces are permeable not only to oxygen, but also to other gases in solution, and in fact some fishes get rid of certain waste products through the gills in the form of ammonia. In fishes that live in sea water, which has a salt concentration higher than that in the fish's body tissues, the gills also act as salt-regulating organs, removing the excess salt that is continually entering the body from outside.

In some fishes part of the gill chamber is modified to serve as an organ for breathing air; this applies particularly to the labyrinth fishes (Anabantidae). The fish takes in atmospheric air at the surface and retains it as a bubble in a special part of the gill chamber, where the tissues gradually remove the oxygen from it. The fish then rises again to the surface and snaps up another bubble of air.

Circulatory system
In fishes the circulatory system is somewhat simpler than in the higher vertebrates that breathe by means of lungs. The veins carry the blood into the thin-walled sinus venosus, whence it passes into the auricle and then into the ventricle of the heart. From there it is pumped into the ventral aorta, from which it travels in branch vessels to the gills where oxygen is received by the blood and carbon dioxide lost. The oxygenated blood is then received into the dorsal aorta, which divides into numerous branches that take it to all parts of the body.

Kidneys and gonads
In most fishes the kidneys are elongated, paired organs lying in the roof of the body cavity above the swimbladder, and immediately below the vertebral column. The urinary ducts from each kidney unite to form a common sinus which empties to the outside via the urinary bladder. This lies just proximal (or internal) to the urogenital opening, which also carries the genital products.

Bony fishes are normally either male or female, and hermaphrodites are rare. The ovaries and testes are paired organs in which the eggs and sperms are formed. The testes are elongated and whitish, on account of their contents, whereas the ovaries are usually reddish. The gonads or genital organs occupy a varying amount of the body cavity, depending upon the breeding period.

In most fishes the eggs and sperms are shed more or less simultaneously and at random and fertilisation takes place externally, in the water. In the live-bearing toothcarps the anal fin of the male is modified to form a copulatory organ (gonopodium), so that the sperms are introduced directly into the female's oviduct, and the eggs are therefore fertilised internally.

THE SENSES

Like all other vertebrate animals, fishes receive stimuli of a physical or chemical nature from their surroundings by means of specially developed sense organs.

Changes in the composition and intensity of the light are picked up by the eyes, acoustic stimuli by the inner ears and pressure changes by the lateral line system. Chemical stimuli are detected by organs of taste (taste buds) and smell (olfactory organs).

Vision

The basic structure of a fish's eye is not significantly different from that of any other vertebrate, but sensitivity to light and visual acuity vary within the group from the total blindness of certain cave-dwelling fishes to the excellent vision of many species that live in clear water or near the surface.

In general, bony fishes lack eyelids and so the eyes cannot be closed. It is characteristic of a fish's eye that the lens is firm and spherical and that it cannot change shape to allow for close and distant vision. Objects can, however, be brought into focus by moving the position of the whole lens in relation to the retina. This is done by a muscle attached to the lower pole of the lens. Few fishes have binocular vision of the type characteristic of man and certain other animals.

Smell

On each side of the head or on top of the snout, fishes have one or two nostrils, usually two, in which case they are separated by a narrow bridge of skin. In bony fishes the olfactory pit is a blind sac, the bottom of which is lined with special sensory cells. These are connected to the front part of the brain, which is well developed in fishes as an olfactory centre.

The sense of smell is particularly well developed in barbs and catfishes, in which 'alarm substances' released from wounded individuals in a school or shoal serve to warn the rest of the group of possible enemies.

Cutaneous senses

Certain fishes from both fresh and sea water can detect temperature differences of as little as 0·03°C (0·05°F). This is done by thin, branched nerves distributed in the epidermis of the fish's body.

Some fishes have a tactile sense. Generally there are no special sensory receptors serving this function, although in the gouramis, for instance, it is possible that the thin pectoral fin filaments may have a tactile function.

Many fishes with poor vision or those living in turbid waters have barbels or similar structures around the mouth, which carry numerous taste buds; these may also occur on the lips, in the pharynx and on the body surface.

The inner ear

The inner ear is the seat of the senses of equilibrium and hearing. The organ of equilibrium in the upper part of the ear consists of the semicircular canals and the utriculus. The lower part of the ear (lagena and sacculus) is the hearing centre and it also plays a part in equilibrium. In bony fishes the three cavities (utriculus, lagena and sacculus) contain small, limy concretions, known as otoliths. The displacement of the otoliths relative to the sensory hairs in these cavities enables the fish to get an idea of its position in space. This is also helped by the retina's perception of light. Thus, gravity will tend to pull the otoliths down, while light from above will act on the lower part of the retina.

Lateral line

The lateral line system consists of a series of dermal canals with numerous small groups of special sensory cells. The canals communicate with the skin surface by tiny pores. The lateral line can be seen in many but not all fishes as a thin line running along each flank. It is, however, very variable in form and extent.

In most fishes the lateral line runs more or less in a curve from behind the head to the root of the tail. In front it joins on to the lateral line system of the head which typically consists of three main branches, one passing over the eye to the tip of the snout, one passing below the eye and on to the snout region, and the third passing behind the eye to the lower jaw.

When water currents or pressure waves strike the surface of the fish, they are transmitted through the mucus in the canals to the sensory cells, which are known as neuromasts. The latter are supplied by branches from four of the cerebral nerves. The lateral line sense is therefore activated by local disturbances caused by small currents or oscillations in the water and this enables the fish to localise prey, enemies or fixed objects, which reflect water waves sent out by the fish itself.

IDENTIFICATION OF FISHES

In order to obtain full enjoyment from his aquarium fishes it is essential that the aquarist should be in a position to identify his fishes. The correct name of a fish will enable him to consult the relevant literature and thus to learn more about how to keep and breed it in the aquarium.

Unlike the zoologist working in a museum, the aquarist has to identify his fish from living material, and this means using external characters, such as the shape of the body and fins, coloration and pattern, the size and appearance of the eyes, the course of the lateral line, the number of barbels and so on. On the other hand, he cannot use scale and fin-ray counts, let alone accurate measurements of the fish's external morphological characters. The aquarist must therefore either rely on the accuracy of a given trade name or undertake to identify the fish with the help of the available illustrations in books and periodicals (often black-and-white photographs). In the vast majority of cases there will be little or no doubt as to the identity of the fish, but problems will arise when he is faced with a fish that is rarely kept in the aquarium.

Fish names

The naming of fishes and of all other animals (also plants) is based on the scientific or Latin name which consists of two parts: a *generic name*, always written with an initial capital letter, and a *specific name*, written with an initial lower case letter, e.g. *Rasbora heteromorpha*. In addition to these two words the scientific literature often gives the name of the person who first described the species and the year in which he did so, in this case Duncker, 1904. The specimen on which the first scientific description of a fish species is based is known as the holotype or type specimen, and according to the *International Rules of Zoological Nomenclature* this specimen must be deposited in a museum collection available to the public. In some cases the scientific or Latin name is followed by the author's name and the date placed in brackets, e.g. *Rasbora einthoveni* (Bleeker, 1851). This means that in 1851 Bleeker described the species but placed it in a different genus, but that this has since been altered. In certain groups there is constant revision of the genera and species. In recent years many well-known aquarium fishes have had a change in the name of their genus, often as a result of investigations of their chromosomes.

Provided that a newly named species is not identical with a species described earlier, it retains its specific name even if it is later transferred to another genus. This does not, of course, prevent geographical races differing in appearance from going under different specific names. There are, in fact, several examples of this. When and if such a mistake is found, the name first published is the valid one. Thus, there is much doubt as to whether the different discus fishes are so-called 'good species' or merely colour varieties of two species. Until a more detailed investigation has taken place, the problem is dealt with by making them into subspecies, see below. The subspecific name is added as a third word after the generic and specific names, e.g. *Symphysodon aequifasciata haraldi*.

The species concept

The smallest commonly employed unit in the system of known animals is known as the *species*. One or more closely related species are grouped together in a *genus* (plural, *genera*). One or more genera then form a *family* and one or more families an *order*. In the case of fishes, the numerous orders are grouped or classified under four *classes*, of which the bony fishes or Osteichthyes are by far the dominant group, and they contain all the species suitable for the home aquarium.

It was formerly the custom to define a 'good zoological species' on the basis of definite external anatomical characters. It is now realised that two species can resemble one another to the point of confusion, and yet be unable to breed with one another or may even have a different chromosome number. So, a species can now be defined as: groups of populations which can potentially or in fact breed with one another, but not with other populations. The older concept of a species was based on external or morphological criteria, whereas the newer concept relies on the genetical or biological background. Of course, most of the older type species, based purely on morphological characters, are also good species from the genetic viewpoint. In recent years it has, however, been discovered, from breeding experiments and chromosome counts, that some morphologically identical individuals are in fact genetically different, and so constitute different species. Conversely, a species based on chromosomal and breeding criteria may split up into two or more morphologically different types and yet these may retain the ability to interbreed.

This brief summary of some of the problems involved in the species concept should, in some measure, explain why the names of many fishes are being changed from time to time as a result of new research on their biology. Such changes of names do, of course, cause confusion, and in the aquarium world this has been particularly evident in the case of the killifishes, the live-bearing toothcarps, and the cichlids.

In addition to these problems involving the scientific naming of fishes the aquarist is also faced with the problem of popular names. In many countries the same fish may be marketed under widely different trade names. The popular names given in this book are only those believed to be well established, and no attempt has been made to invent new ones.

Photographic identification of fishes

Nowadays it should frequently be possible to identify living fishes from photographs of adult, sexually mature specimens. This does, of course, require that the picture is sharp enough so that it is possible to count the scales and fin-rays and to measure the different parts of the body. A good, sharp colour photograph can, in fact be an invaluable help in the identification of many fishes.

Identification of dead fishes

The most reliable way of getting a fish identified is to send a dead specimen to a zoological museum, but if every aquarist did this the staff of such institutions would be quite unable to cope. It is however, possible for the serious aquarist to identify his fishes by consulting the larger systematic works (see bibliography) which give scale and fin counts and body measurements for the different species.

Note: In the illustrations the sex of a fish is denoted by the appropriate zoological sign: ♂ = male ♀ = female

Pantodontidae
1. Pantodon
   buchholzi
Notopteridae
2. Xenomystus
   nigri

Mormyridae
3. Gnathonemus petersii
4. Marcusenius
   schilthuisiae
5. Campylomormyrus
   tamandua

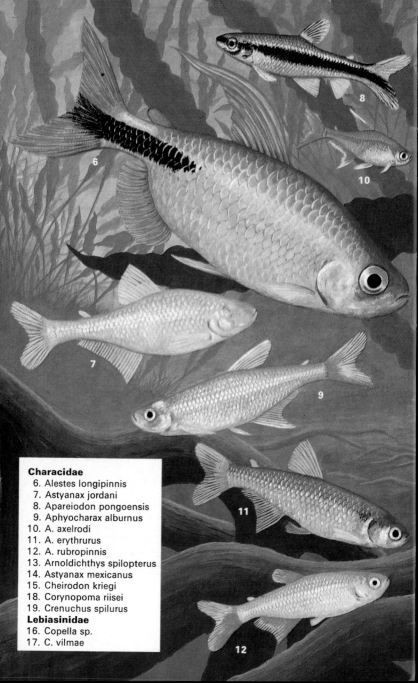

Characidae
  6. *Alestes longipinnis*
  7. *Astyanax jordani*
  8. *Apareiodon pongoensis*
  9. *Aphyocharax alburnus*
10. *A. axelrodi*
11. *A. erythrurus*
12. *A. rubropinnis*
13. *Arnoldichthys spilopterus*
14. *Astyanax mexicanus*
15. *Cheirodon kriegi*
18. *Corynopoma riisei*
19. *Crenuchus spilurus*
Lebiasinidae
16. *Copella sp.*
17. *C. vilmae*

Characidae
20. Ctenobrycon spilurus
21. Ephippicharax orbicularis
22. Glandulocauda inaequalis
23. Gymnocorymbus ternetzi
24. Hasemania marginata
25. Hemigrammus armstrongi
26. H. caudovittatus
27. H. gracilis
28. H. hyanuary
29. H. marginatus
30. H. ocellifer
31. H. pulcher
32. Petitella georgiae
33. Hemigrammus unilineatus

Characidae
53. Ladigesia roloffi
54. Megalamphodus megalopterus
55. M. sweglesi
56. Phenacogrammus interruptus
57. Alestopetersius caudalis
58. Boehlkea fredcochui
59. Moenkhausia oligolepis
60. M. pittieri
61. M. sanctaefilomenae
62. Nematobrycon palmeri
63. N. lacortei

59

60

61

62

63

62 ♀

Characidae
64. Pristella riddlei
65. Pseudocorynopoma doriae
67. Thayeria boehlkei
68. T. ifati
69. T. obliqua
70. T. sanctaemariae
Lebiasinidae
66. Pyrrhulina vittata
Anostomidae
71. Abramites microcephalus
72. Anostomus anostomus
Chilodontidae
73. Chilodus punctatus

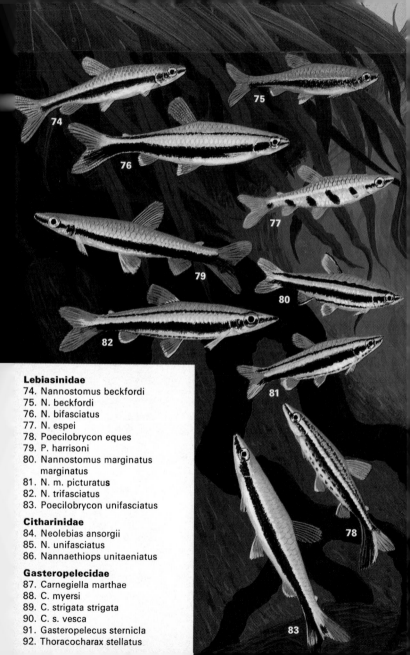

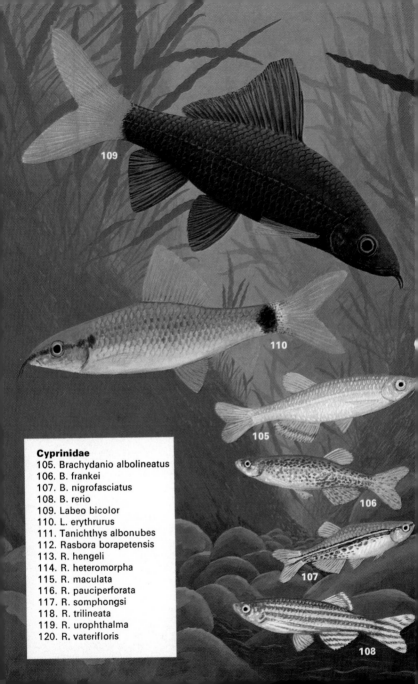

Cyprinidae
105. Brachydanio albolineatus
106. B. frankei
107. B. nigrofasciatus
108. B. rerio
109. Labeo bicolor
110. L. erythrurus
111. Tanichthys albonubes
112. Rasbora borapetensis
113. R. hengeli
114. R. heteromorpha
115. R. maculata
116. R. pauciperforata
117. R. somphongsi
118. R. trilineata
119. R. urophthalma
120. R. vaterifloris

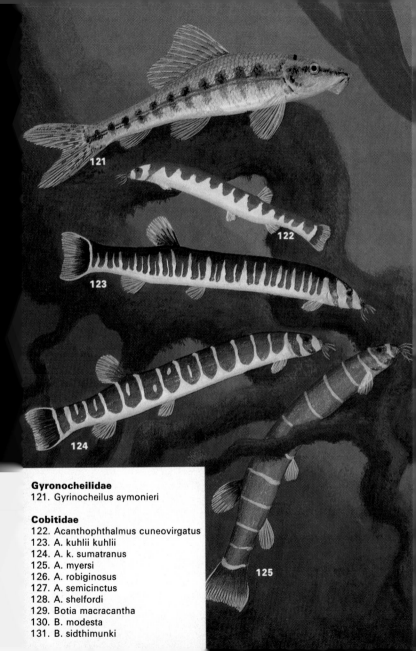

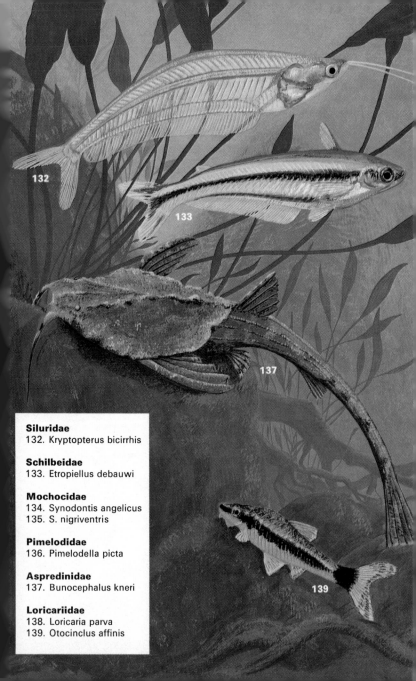

Siluridae
132. Kryptopterus bicirrhis

Schilbeidae
133. Etropiellus debauwi

Mochocidae
134. Synodontis angelicus
135. S. nigriventris

Pimelodidae
136. Pimelodella picta

Aspredinidae
137. Bunocephalus kneri

Loricariidae
138. Loricaria parva
139. Otocinclus affinis

Callichthyidae
140. Brochis coeruleus
141. Corydoras aeneus
142. C. arcuatus
143. C. axelrodi
144. C. barbatus
145. C. caudimaculatus
146. C. elegans
147. C. melini
148. C. metae
149. C. myersi
150. C. paleatus
151. C. schultzei

Callichthyidae
152. Corydoras cochui
153. C. haraldschultzi
154. C. hastatus
155. C. julii
156. C. melanistius
157. C. punctatus
158. C. pygmaeus
159. C. reticulatus
160. C. schwartzi
161. C. undulatus
162. Dianema urostriata
163. Hoplosternum thoracatum

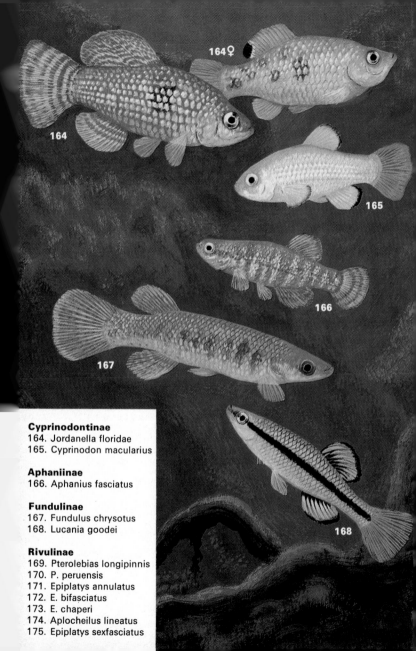

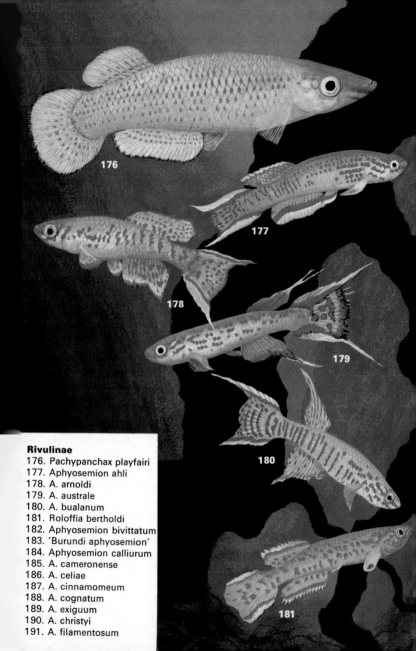

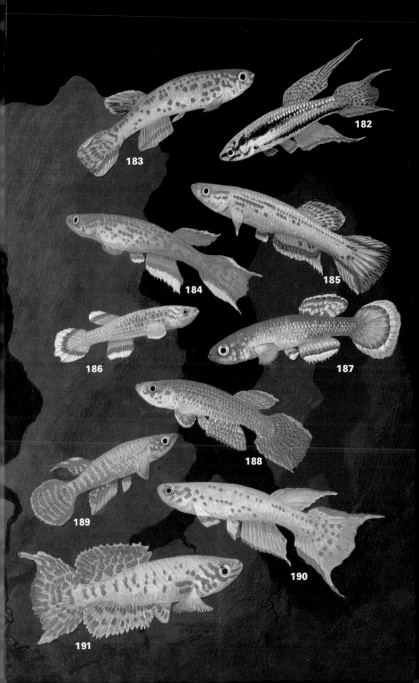

Rivulinae
204. Austrofundulus dolichopterus
205. Cynolebias belottii
206. C. nigripinnis
207. C. whitei
208. Nothobranchius guentheri
209. N. palmquisti
210. N. rachovii
211. Fundulosoma thierryi

Procatopodinae
212. Procatopus nototaenia
213. Aplocheilichthys macrophthalmus
214. A. schioetzi

Oryziatinae
215. Oryzias javanicus

208

209

210

211

213

214

212

215 ♀

215

Poeciliidae
216. Belonesox belizanus
217. Gambusia affinis affinis
218. G. a. holbrooki
219. Girardinus metallicus
220. Heterandria formosa
221. Phalloceros caudimaculatus reticulatus
222. Poecilia melanogaster
223. P. nigrofasciata

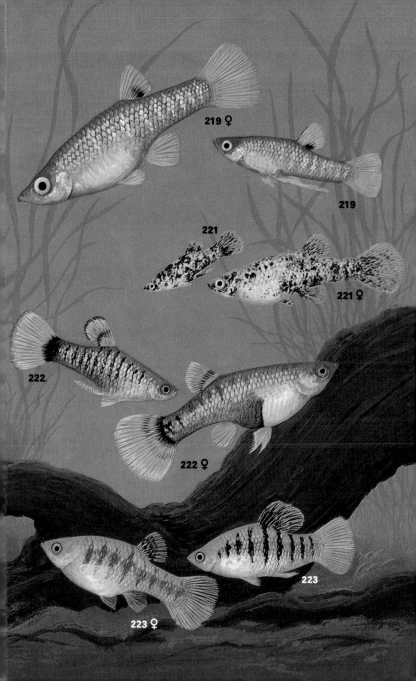

219 ♀

219

221

221 ♀

222

222 ♀

223

223 ♀

Poeciliidae
224. *Poecilia reticulata*

225 ♀

226 ♀

226

Poeciliidae
225. Poecilia sphenops
226. P. velifera
227. P. vittata
228. Priapella intermedia

225

225 a

225 b

227

227 ♀

228

228 ♀

229

229 ♀

229

Poeciliidae
229. Xiphophorus helleri helleri
230. X. maculatus
231. X. variatus

229

230 ♀

230

230

230

231 ♀

231

231

Anablepidae
232. Anableps anableps

Hemiramphidae
233. Dermogenys pusillus

Syngnathidae
234. Syngnathus pulchellus

Centrarchidae
235. Elassoma evergladei
236. Enneacanthus chaetodon

Centropomidae
237. Chanda ranga
238. Gynochanda filamentosa

236

237

238

238 ♀

Toxotidae
239. Toxotes jaculatrix

Monodactylidae
240. Monodactylus argenteus
241. M. sebae

Scatophagidae
242. Scatophagus argus

241

242

Badidae
243. Badis badis
244. B. b. burmanicus
Nandidae
245. Monocirrhus polyacanthus
246. Nandus nandus
247. Polycentropsis abbreviata
248. Polycentrus schomburgki

246

248

248

248 ♀

250

251 ♀

Cichlidae
249. Aequidens curviceps
250. A. itanyi
251. A. pulcher
252. A. maronii

252

49

251

Cichlidae
253. Apistogramma agassizi
254. A. cacatuoides
255. A. ortmanni
256. A. reitzigi
257. A. trifasciatum haraldschultzi
258. A. wickleri

256

256♀

257

257♀

258

258♀

Cichlidae
259. Astronotus ocellatus
260. Cichlasoma octofasciatum
261. C. citrinellum
262. C. festivum
263. C. meeki
264. C. nigrofasciatum

265

266

270

Cichlidae
265. Cichlasoma spilurum
266. Crenicara filamentosa
267. Geophagus jurupari
268. Apistogramma ramirezi
269. Nannacara anomala
270. N. taenia

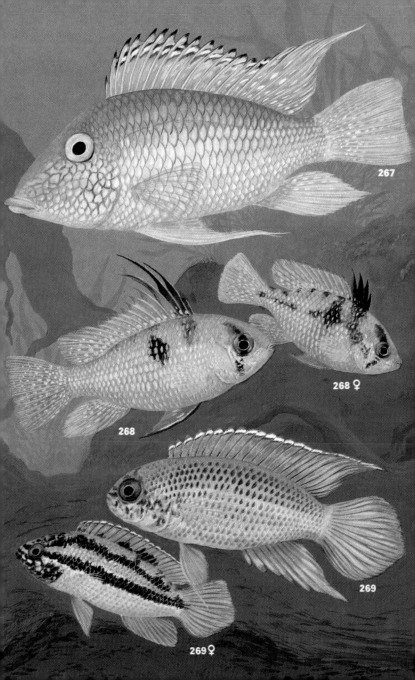

267

268 ♀

268

269

269 ♀

Cichlidae
271. Pterophyllum scalare

♀

272

Cichlidae
272. Symphysodon discus
273. S. aequifasciata axelrodi
274. S. a. haraldi

Cichlidae
275. Etroplus maculatus
276. Haplochromis burtoni
277. Hemichromis bimaculatus
278. Hemihaplochromis multicolor
279. Nanochromis nudiceps

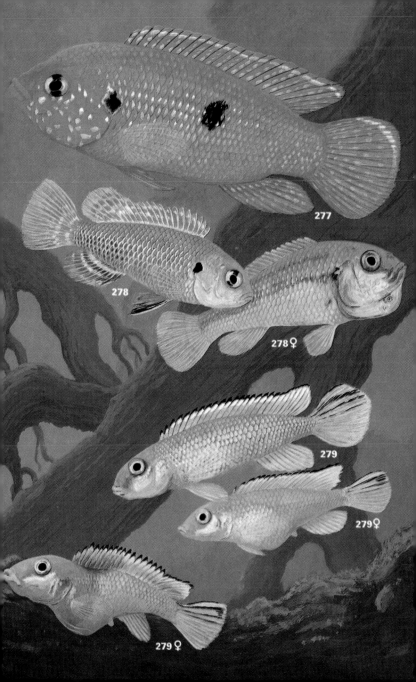

277

278

278 ♀

279

279 ♀

279 ♀

Cichlidae
280. Thysia ansorgii
281. Chromidotilapia guntheri
282. Pelmatochromis thomasi
283. Pelvicachromis pulcher
284. Steatocranus casuarius

283

283 ♀

284

285

285 ♀

287

Cichlidae
285. Labeotropheus fuelleborni
286. L. trewavasae
287. Labidochromis vellicans
288. Melanochromis
      melanopterus
289. Pseudotropheus auratus

286

288

289

289 ♀

Cichlidae
290. Pseudotropheus elongatus
291. Melanochromis vermivorus
292. Iodotropheus sprengerae
293. Pseudotropheus tropheops
294. P. zebra

294 a

294 b

294 ♀

Cichlidae
295. Tanganicodus irsacae
296. Julidochromis marlieri
297. J. ornatus
298. Lamprologus congolensis
299. L. brichardi
300. Tropheus duboisi
301. T. moorei

298

299

300

301

Gobiidae
302. Brachygobius aggregatus
303. B. nunus
304. B. xanthozona
305. Periophthalmus barbarus
306. P. koelreuteri
307. Stigmatogobius sadanundio

Anabantidae
308. Belontia signata
309. Betta bellica
310. B. splendens

310 a

310

310 ♀

310

310

Anabantidae
311. Colisa chuna
312. C. fasciata
313. C. labiosa
314. C. lalia
315. Macropodus concolor
316. M. cupanus dayi
317. M. opercularis

312

313

313 ♀

311

Anabantidae
318. Ctenopoma acutirostre
319. C. ansorgii
320. C. congicum
321. C. fasciolatum
322. C. nanum
323. C. ocellatum

321

322

323

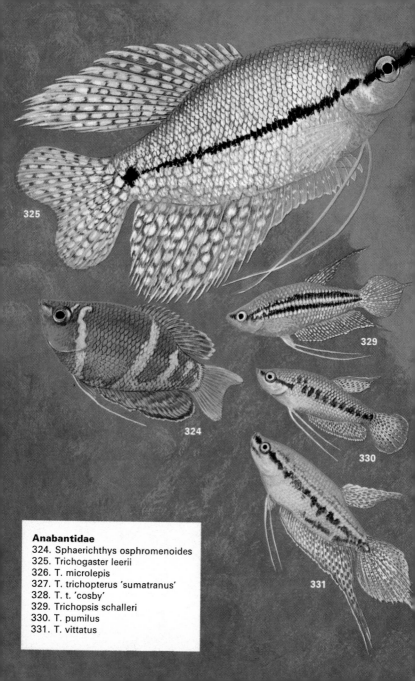

Anabantidae
324. Sphaerichthys osphromenoides
325. Trichogaster leerii
326. T. microlepis
327. T. trichopterus 'sumatranus'
328. T. t. 'cosby'
329. Trichopsis schalleri
330. T. pumilus
331. T. vittatus

326

327

328

Luciocephalidae
332. Luciocephalus pulcher

Atherinidae
333. Bedotia geayi
334. Melanotaenia maccullochi
335. M. nigrans
336. Telmatherina ladigesi

332

336

336 ♀

335

Tetraodontidae
337. Carinotetraodon somphongsi
338. Tetraodon fluviatilis
339. T. palembangensis

Canthigasteridae
340. Canthigaster margaritatus
341. C. valentini

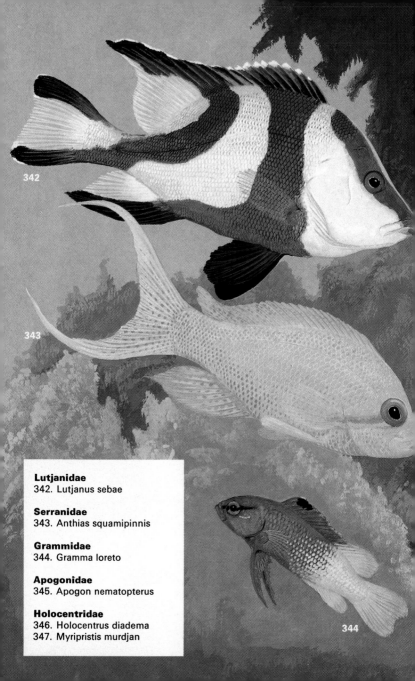

342

343

Lutjanidae
342. Lutjanus sebae

Serranidae
343. Anthias squamipinnis

Grammidae
344. Gramma loreto

Apogonidae
345. Apogon nematopterus

Holocentridae
346. Holocentrus diadema
347. Myripristis murdjan

344

345

346

347

Sciaenidae
348. Equetus acuminatus
349. E. lanceolatus

Pomadasyidae
350. Plectorhynchus chaetodonoides

Chaetodontidae
351. Heniochus acuminatus
352. Chelmon rostratus
353. Forcipiger flavissimus

350

352

353

Zanclidae
354. Zanclus canescens

Chaetodontidae
355. Chaetodon auriga
356. C. chrysurus
357. C. collaris
358. C. kleinii

356

358

357

359

360

Chaetodontidae
359. Chaetodon ephippium
360. C. larvatus
361. C. lunula
362. C. melannotus
363. C. ocellatus

359

361

362

363

Chaetodontidae
364. Chaetodon ornatissimus
365. C. xanthocephalus

Pomancanthidae
366. Chaetodontoplus mesoleucus
367. Pocanthus annularis
368. P. semicirculatus (young)
369. P. imperator (young)

366

365

367

372

373

371

Pomacanthidae
374. Euxiphipops navarchus
375. E. xanthometopon
376. Centropyge bispinosus
377. C. fisheri
378. C. flavissimus
379. C. tibicen

375

377

379

Pomacentridae
380. Pomacentrus annulatus
381. P. caeruleus
382. Abudefduf parasema
383. Chromis caeruleus
384. C. chromis
385. C. dimidiatus
386. Abudefduf behni
387. A. oxyodon

Pomacentridae
388. Abudefduf saxatilis
389. Dascyllus aruanus
390. D. melanurus
391. D. reticulatus
392. D. trimaculatus
393. Microspathodon chrysurus
394. Amphiprion biaculeatus

Pomacentridae
395. *Amphiprion sandaracinos*
396. *A. allardi*
397. *A. chrysopterus*
398. *A. frenatus*
399. *A. ephippium*
400. *A. polymnus*
401. *A. ocellaris*
402. *A. perideraion*
403. *A. chrysopterus*

399

400

402

403

401

Labridae
404. Bodianus axillaris
405. Coris aygula
406. C. gaimardi
407. C. gaimardi
408. C. julis
409. Hemigymnus melapterus

406

407

408

409

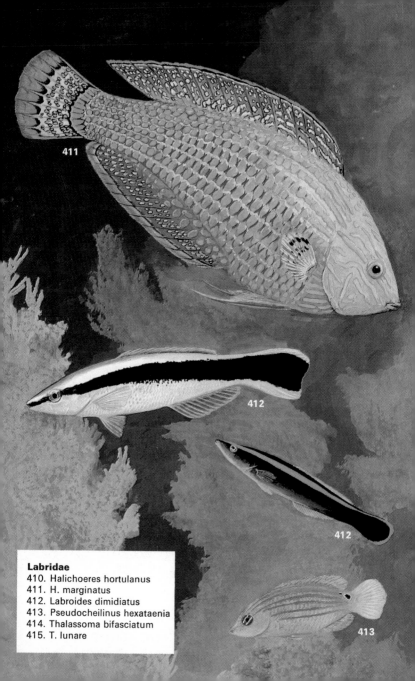

Labridae
410. Halichoeres hortulanus
411. H. marginatus
412. Labroides dimidiatus
413. Pseudocheilinus hexataenia
414. Thalassoma bifasciatum
415. T. lunare

410

414

414

415

415

Acanthuridae
416. Acanthurus glaucopareius
417. A. leucosternon
418. A. lineatus
419. Paracanthurus hepatus

Acanthuridae
420. Acanthurus achilles
421. Zebrasoma veliferum
422. Z. xanthurum

Scaridae
423. Scarus frenatus

422

423

Balistidae
424. Balistapus undulatus
425. Balistoides niger
426. Sufflamen chrysoptera
427. Melichthys vidua

424

427

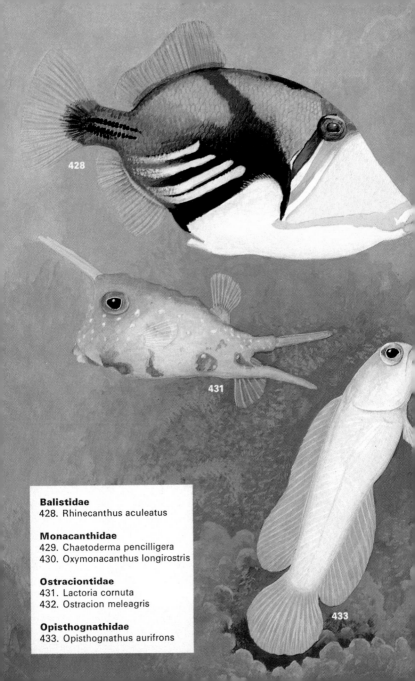

Balistidae
428. Rhinecanthus aculeatus

Monacanthidae
429. Chaetoderma pencilligera
430. Oxymonacanthus longirostris

Ostraciontidae
431. Lactoria cornuta
432. Ostracion meleagris

Opisthognathidae
433. Opisthognathus aurifrons

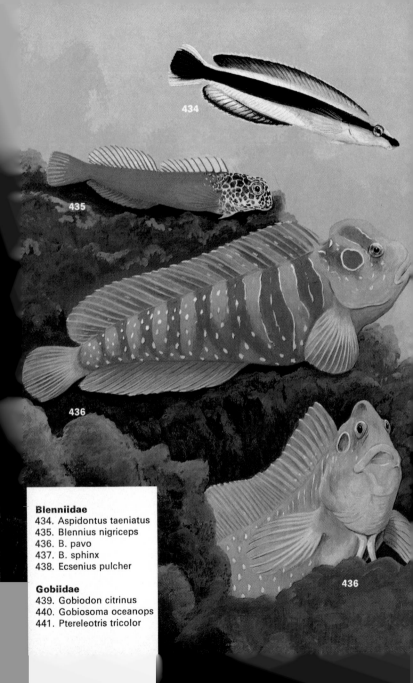

Blenniidae
434. Aspidontus taeniatus
435. Blennius nigriceps
436. B. pavo
437. B. sphinx
438. Ecsenius pulcher

Gobiidae
439. Gobiodon citrinus
440. Gobiosoma oceanops
441. Ptereleotris tricolor

Ephippidae
442. Platax orbicularis
443. P. pinnatus
444. P. teira

Scorpaenidae
445. Dendrochirus brachypterus
446. Pterois radiata
447. P. volitans

445

446

Callionymidae
448. Synchiropus splendidus

Plotosidae
449. Plotosus lineatus

Centriscidae
450. Aeoliscus strigatus

Syngnathidae
451. Dunckerocampus caulleryi

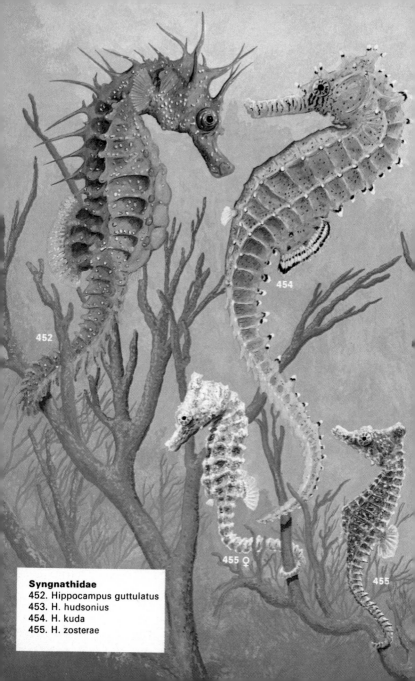

Syngnathidae
452. Hippocampus guttulatus
453. H. hudsonius
454. H. kuda
455. H. zosterae

453

453 ♀

453

E

16 ♂

F

C

66 ♂

320 ♀

A

60 ♀

K

278 ♀

56 ♀

98 ♀

B

236 ♂

167 ♀

D

J1.

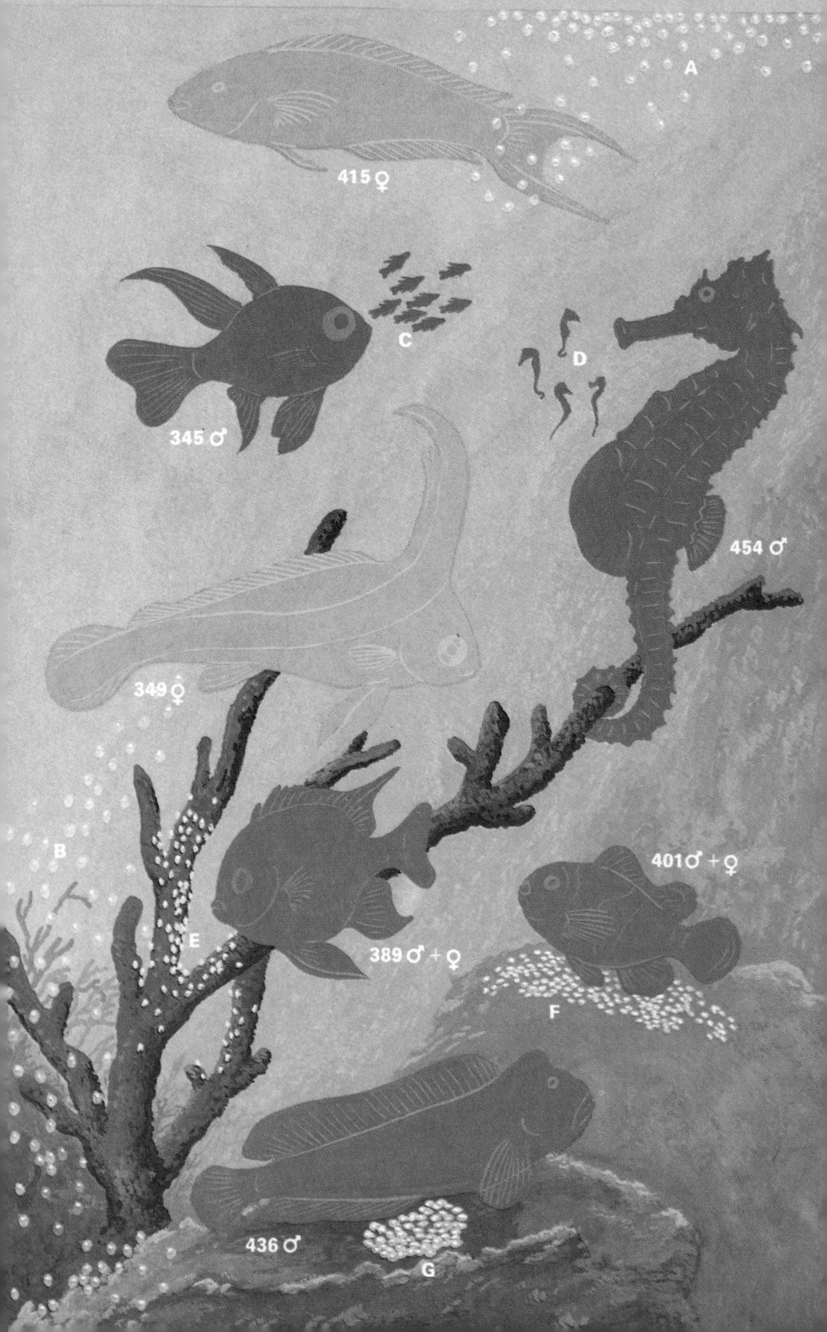
A
415 ♀
C
D
345 ♂
454 ♂
349 ♀
B
401 ♂ + ♀
E
389 ♂ + ♀
F
436 ♂
G

DESCRIPTIONS OF THE FISHES

Specie names: where there is a variance in American and British classification or nomenclature both names are given. The American name appears first and the British name is given directly below it in square brackets.

FRESHWATER FISHES

Pantodontidae
Butterflyfish
A small family, with only one known species. Widespread in tropical Africa from Nigeria to the Zaïre (formerly called Congo) rain-forest. Most closely related to the osteoglossids or bony-tongues.

1. *Pantodon buchholzi*
   Butterflyfish
10 cm (3¾ in.). Sex difference: back edge of the anal fin concave in the male, straight in the female. In large areas of still water, with dense vegetation. A typical surface-living fish which feeds mainly on insects that fall onto the water. When hunting flying insects it can make low jumps out of the water, but cannot fly.

This rather stationary fish should be kept in a large shallow tank planted with patches of vegetation; it is not very particular about the type of water. Temperature 25–29°C (77–84°F). These fish should be fed on a varied insect diet: flies, small mealworms, mosquito or gnat larvae and ant pupae, as well as small fish. They will only take food from the surface or from the upper water layers.

For breeding, the tank should be shallow with a content of over 80 litres (21·1 U.S. gals), with shelter provided by floating plants or overhanging leaves. The bottom should not be too pale and the water soft and slightly acid. Temperature: 28°C (82°F).

Spawning starts with several sham matings, in which the male holds the female's back firmly with his ventral fins. In true mating the male approaches the side of the female and both fish make a series of rapid turns during which the female releases 3–8 eggs, which rise to the surface. The pair spawn daily over a long period. The eggs, which are dark, hatch in 36–48 hours. The fry at first have a large yolk sac. They are difficult to feed as they keep close to the surface. It is best to give them *Cyclops* nauplii which can be moved round in the water by the aeration system. The water in the rearing tank should be kept shallow. After about three weeks the young can break through the surface layer and take from it food such as springtails, aphids and small fruit-flies. The young grow slowly and are not fully grown until they are at least a year old.

Notopteridae
Knifefishes
This family has only two genera with five known species. They are all elongated, with rudimentary ventral and dorsal fins. The very long anal fin is fused with the caudal fin, and the undulating movements of the

structure thus formed can propel the fish forwards or backwards. Knifefishes live in still or slow-flowing waters, where they remain hidden by day among vegetation or under the banks of the river, often in small shoals, each taking up a characteristic oblique resting position with the head down. They come out at night to search for food. The swimbladder acts as an accessory respiratory organ and at intervals the fish takes in a mouthful of air at the surface. Large specimens are often aggressive and predatory. Not yet bred in captivity.

2. *Xenomystus nigri*
African Knifefish
20 cm (7¾ in.). Upper tributaries of the Nile to Liberia. The smallest of the known species. Sex differences: none known. Lacks a dorsal fin.

Should be kept in large tanks with patches of dense vegetation, but is not particular about the type of water. Several specimens can be kept together, and under such conditions may quickly become quite tame. A rather voracious fish that will take all kinds of live food, as well as raw fish flesh, calf and pig heart and the usual dried food preparations.

Mormyridae
Elephant Trunk Fishes
A large family of African fishes, whose systematics have been little investigated. Most of the species are inconspicuous blue-black or brown fishes. The shape of the head varies from one like that of an anteater to that of a sperm whale. The caudal peduncle is usually slender, the caudal fin much indented, the eyes small and the skin thick with very small scales. All the species are crepuscular, and live in muddy, slow-flowing waters. Even the ancient Egyptians were interested in these curious fishes, and

ascribed magical properties to them. In our time, the mormyrids have become of scientific interest because of their ability to produce weak electric pulses which are used in orientation. They have electric organs which continuously send out a weak current of *c.* 3–10 volts at a frequency of 300 cycles per second. In this way a spherical electric field is produced round the body of the fish. Objects in the immediate vicinity will produce changes in this electric field, distorting it from the normal, and these changes are perceived by the fish. The sensitivity to voltage drop and changes in current is comparable to the ability of the eye to react to a single quantum of light. In addition to being able to perceive changes in the strength of the electric field, these fishes can also use their electric sense to estimate the size and form of an object with very great accuracy and also the direction in which it is moving.

In association with this almost unique system the mormyrids also have the largest brain of any fish, relative to their size. This is reflected in several other aspects of their behaviour, and their ability to learn is therefore much greater than that of most other fishes. It is not uncommon to see mormyrids playing with small twigs, which they balance on their snout, and there are descriptions of individuals which play with balls of aluminium foil.

Mormyrids can be very aggressive towards one another and they should therefore be kept singly or in very large tanks. They thrive in almost all types of water. Temperature 22–27°C (72–81°F). They can be fed on earthworms, *Tubifex* and whiteworms, and will also quickly become acclimatised to taking dead food. None of the species has yet bred in captivity.

154

3. *Gnathonemus petersii*
   [*Gnathonemus petersi*]
20–25 cm (7¾–10 in.). West Africa, Zaïre and Cameroun. The elongated lower jaw is modified to form a movable digging organ. A very shy species, which needs good hiding-places in the form of roots and dense vegetation.

4. *Marcusenius schilthuisiae*
   [*Gnathonemus schilthuisiae*]
10 cm (3¾ in.). Africa, Zaïre. One of the most peaceful species; can be kept in a small shoal when young.

5. *Campylomormyrus tamandua*
   [*Gnathonemus tamandua*]
20 cm (7¾ in.). West Africa, Nigeria and Zaïre.

Characidae
Characins
A very large family distributed in South, Central and southern North America, as well as in Africa; it contains many of the most popular aquarium fishes. Most species are essentially shoaling or schooling fishes, which occur in running waters. Almost all have an adipose fin, in contrast to the barbs they lack barbels and possess teeth in the jaws. The adaptive abilities of the different species are very variable and so are the conditions in which they should be kept in the aquarium (see under the individual species). They are almost all predatory and should be fed mainly on animal food. In addition to the small, peaceful species described here the family also contains the piranhas which are feared in South America on account of their sharp teeth and relatively large size. When attacking in a shoal they are able to kill swimming animals and reduce them to a skeleton in a remarkably short time. They have never become widely distributed among aquarists, although the true Piranha has bred in captivity. The male fans out a depression in the bottom, round which he forms a wall of algae and plant debris. The large, amber-yellow eggs and the fry are guarded until the latter are free-swimming.

6. *Alestes longipinnis*
   Long-finned Characin
10–15 cm (3¾–6 in.). West Africa. A river fish. Sex differences: dorsal fin rays elongated in the male. Adipose fin purplish-red in the male, transparent in the female. Should be kept in a large tank with good water circulation. Omnivorous, but prefers insect food. A good jumper, so the tank cover glass should be close-fitting. Breeding in captivity has not been described.

7. *Astyanax jordani*
   [*Anoptichthys jordani*]
   Blind Cave Characin
   [Blind Cavefish]
6–8 cm (2¼–3 in.). Mexico, in subterranean watercourses. Descended from a form of *Astyanax mexicanus* or *A. fasciatus*. Lacks dark pigment and has poor vision, but this is compensated for by the very well developed lateral line system. Not particular about the type of water Temperature: 18–22°C (64–72°F). Need not necessarily be kept in a darkened tank. For breeding the water should be soft (*c.* 8–12° DH). The eggs are laid just below the water surface, and they hatch in 3–4 days. The young are free-swimming after a further two days, and they then grow rapidly.

8. *Apareiodon pongoensis*
   Pongo pongo
5 cm (2 in.). Peru, Pongo de Menseriche. Sex differences: none described. According to descriptions in the

literature this species keeps to the lower water layers and from time to time swims round in circles with a diameter of *c.* 10 cm (4 in.). Breeding unknown in the aquarium.

9. *Aphyocharax alburnus*
7 cm (2¾ in.). Marañon, southern Brazil, Rio Paraná. Sex difference: male slenderer than female. For care and biology see No. 12.

10. *Aphyocharax axelrodi*
3 cm (1¼ in.). Distribution not known in detail. Sex differences: male slenderer and more brightly coloured than female. For care and biology see No. 12.

11. *Aphyocharax erythrurus*
6–7 cm (2¼–2¾ in.). Western Guyana. A synonym of *Aphyocharax alburnus* (according to Gery). Sex difference: male slenderer than the female. For care and biology see No. 12.

12. *Aphyocharax rubropinnis*
Bloodfin
4·5–5 cm (2 in.). Argentina, Rio La Plata. Sex differences: male slenderer than female; he also has small hooks on the anal fin which cannot be seen with the naked eye, but they often become entangled in the net when the fish is being caught. Lively, shoaling fish which should be kept in groups of 10–12 or more in a spacious tank. Temperature 24–25°C (75–77°F). Does very well in medium hard or hard water. Spawning often takes place in the early hours of the morning in open water just below the surface, and the whole group may take part. A single female will lay 300–500 small, transparent eggs which hatch in 30 hours at 25°C (77°F). The young are free-swimming after 3–4 days. They should be fed during the first week on *Paramecium*,

rotifers or *Cyclops* nauplii, and after then on *Artemia* nauplii. They grow rapidly. The breeding tank should have shallow water, a breeding trap and a few fine-leaved plants as these fish are bad egg-eaters. The water type is not of great importance. The genus *Aphyocharax* has about twenty known species.

13. *Arnoldichthys spilopterus*
Red-eyed Characin
7–8 cm (2¾–3 in.). West Africa, Lagos to the Niger Delta. Sex differences: male more brightly coloured and with the rear edge of the anal fin very convex. A typical, shoaling, rain-forest fish, which should be kept in large well-planted tanks with good water circulation and soft, slightly acid water. They keep mainly to the upper water layers and much of their food is taken at the surface. Temperature: 26–28°C (79–82°F). The tank cover should be close-fitting as this species is a good jumper. Rearing results have not been reported but breeding is probably as for No. 56.

14. *Astyanax mexicanus*
9–10 cm (3½–3¾ in.). Texas to Panama. Sex differences: male slenderer and more brightly coloured than female. Care and breeding as for No. 12. Spawning takes place in the middle water layers, either in open water or among fine-leaved plants. In the aquarium the brassy sheen of the wild-caught fish disappears even in the first generation.

15. *Cheirodon kriegi*
5 cm (2 in.). South America, upper Rio Paraguay to Rio San Francisco. Care and breeding as for No. 12. This species is now regarded as being the same as *Cheirodon piaba*. There is, in general, some disagreement as regards the naming of species in the genus *Cheirodon*.

Lebiasinidae U.S.A.
Characidae Britain

16. Copella sp.
[*Copeina arnoldi*]
Spraying Characin
Male 8 cm (3 in.), female 6 cm (2¼ in.). Lower Amazon, Rio Pará. A hardy, omnivorous, surface-living fish, which spawns above the water surface on overhanging leaves. Spawning starts with the male swimming across the female. Both fish then rise vertically to the surface. Positioned close together the pair will then leap up, under a leaf (or the tank cover), sometimes jumping to a height of 7–8 cm (3 in.). There they hold on briefly to the leaf with the pectoral and ventral fins and the lower jaw. With her belly pressed close to the underside of the leaf the female lays 10–20 eggs and then falls back into the water. The male immediately sheds sperms over the eggs and drops down into the water. Mating is repeated several times until the female has laid 50–150 eggs; spawning does not take place at each jump. The male then beats the water surface with his tail and splashes water over the eggs, thus preventing them from drying out. At 26°C (79°F) the eggs hatch in about 24 hours and the fry fall down into the water, where they become free-swimming in 3 days. The young have a very small mouth and so must be fed on tiny live food, such as *Paramecium*. The parents should be removed when the eggs hatch.

If a breeding pair has spawned on the cover glass of the tank the eggs can be carefully scraped off with a razor blade and put into a small container with water 6–7 cm (2½ in.) deep. They develop just as well under water as above.

After about a week the young can take *Artemia*. This species is not particular as regards the constitution of the water, but it should not be kept at temperatures below 24°C (75°F).

17. Copella vilmae
Male 7 cm (2¾ in.), female 6 cm (2¼ in.). Upper Amazon at Leticia. Care and rearing as for No. 16, but the eggs are laid on large underwater leaves.

Characidae

18. Corynopoma riisei
Swordtail Characin
7 cm (2¾ in.). Northern Venezuela and Trinidad. Sex differences: in the male the fins are larger and more elongated and each gill cover has an appendage that is up to 3 cm (1¼ in.) in length. The illustration shows a male of the wild form. There is also a creamy-white aquarium strain. These are attractive, omnivorous, shoaling fish, which thrive in a medium-sized tank, preferably in medium-hard or hard water that is kept in motion and at a temperature of 22–25°C (72–77°F). Before spawning the male dances round the female, and spreads out his unpaired fins. He then swings out the gill cover appendages at right angles to the body, so that their golden and black extremities quiver in front of the female. During this characteristic type of courtship the male transfers his sperm in the form of a little sperm packet (spermatophore) into the oviduct of the female. Subsequently and without the presence of the male the female will lay a varying number of eggs on the underside of water plant leaves. The young fish can be reared as described for No. 12.

19. *Crenuchus spilurus*
Sailfin Characin
6 cm (2¼ in.). Western Guyana and the central Amazon region. Sex differences: anal and dorsal fins larger in male than in female, and the tip of the dorsal fin is pointed in the male, rounded in the female; also the male has a pattern of dots on the caudal fin which is lacking in the female. A peaceful, very shy species that should be kept in a well-planted tank of the rain-forest type (see No. 35), that is not too small, and fed preferably on live food. These fish practise brood protection: the eggs are laid in a clump of 40–60, hidden in a hole or on the underside of roots or large leaves. They hatch in about 36 hours at 25°C (77°F). The young are free-swimming after a further 5–6 days. They are small and for the first week should be fed on *Paramecium* or *Cyclops* nauplii. The young are sensitive and so rearing is difficult and will only succeed in soft, rain-forest water. The breeding biology has not been described in detail. This species is rarely seen on the market.

20. *Ctenobrycon spilurus*
Silver Tetra
8 cm (3 in.). Northern South America, near the coasts. Sex differences: the male is smaller and slenderer than the female. A hardy, shoaling fish which should be kept in a tank with a capacity of over 100 litres (26½ U.S. gals). It does very well in any type of water and is very prolific, the female laying up to 1,000 eggs at a time. The young should be reared as for No. 12.

21. *Ephippicharax orbicularis*
12 cm (4¾ in.). Large areas of tropical South America. No reliable sex differences. Aquarium conditions as for No. 20.

22. *Glandulocauda inaequalis*
Male 6 cm (2¼ in.), female 4·5 cm (1¾ in.). South America, Porto Alegre, Rio Grande do Sul. Aquarium conditions as for No. 20. In mating the male transfers a spermatophore into the female, who then lays batches of 5–6 eggs at a time. These are deposited on the underside of leaves with the help of the elongated, tubular genital papilla. Breeding as for No. 18.

23. *Gymnocorymbus ternetzi*
Black Tetra
6–7 cm (2¼–2¾ in.). South America, Rio Paraguay and Rio Negro. Sex differences: male slenderer and more brightly coloured than female. Peaceful, omnivorous fish which do best when kept in a small group. They are most attractive when young, for the deep black pattern disappears with age. Breeding biology as for No. 20. In recent years a veil-tailed form of this species has been developed.

24. *Hasemania marginata*
4 cm (1½ in.). South-east Brazil. Sex differences: male slenderer and more brightly coloured than female. This species has no adipose fin. Care and breeding as for No. 12.

25. *Hemigrammus armstrongi*
Golden Tetra
4·5 cm (1¾ in.). Western Guyana. Sex differences: male slenderer than female, and with a brighter golden sheen and more red in the fins. Care and breeding as for No. 12.

26. *Hemigrammus caudovittatus*
Buenos Aires Tetra
7 cm (2¾ in.). South America, Rio La Plata and its tributaries. Sex differ-

158

ences: male slenderer and more brightly coloured than female; in addition the fins of the female are less pigmented than those of the male. Should be kept in a tank with a capacity of over 80 litres (21 U.S. gals). Care and breeding as for No. 12.

27. *Hemigrammus gracilis*
[[*Hemigrammus erythrozonus*]
Glowlight Tetra
4·5 cm (1¾ in.). Guyana. Sex differences: male slenderer, a little smaller and more intensely coloured than the female. An attractive small tetra which should be kept in groups of ten or more. It does well in all types of water. It breeds successfully in small tanks with fine-leaved plants, e.g. Java Moss (*Vesicularia*), a substrate of sphagnum moss and soft (rain-forest) water, see No. 35. However, most aquarium strains will gradually become accustomed to breeding in ordinary hard mains water. Up to 300 eggs are laid at a time. The young should be reared as for No. 12.

28. *Hemigrammus hyanuary*
4 cm (1½ in.). Lake Hyanuary, near the town of Manaos, where the Rio Negro runs into the Amazon. Sex differences: male slenderer and more intensely coloured than female. This species is best kept as a group in a rain-forest aquarium, but will also do well in hard water. It will breed in tanks of the type described under No. 27, but preferably not under 20 litres (5¼ U.S. gals) capacity. During spawning the male swims right under the female, so that his dorsal fin touches her anal fin. Shortly afterwards he moves up to the side of the female, and the eggs are laid in batches over a period of a few hours. Not a particularly prolific species.

The young should be reared as described under Nos. 12 and 35.

29. *Hemigrammus marginatus*
8 cm (3 in.). Venezuela. Sex difference: dorsal and anal fins with white tips in male only. Care and breeding as for the preceding species.

30. *Hemigrammus ocellifer*
Beacon Fish
4·5 cm (1¾ in.). Amazon region and Guyana. Sex differences: male slenderer and more intensely coloured than female. An attractive and hardy shoaling fish which does not require any special type of water. Care and breeding as for No. 12. This is a very prolific fish. which should not be bred in tanks with a capacity of less than 50 litres (13¼ U.S. gals).

31. *Hemigrammus pulcher*
Pretty Tetra
6 cm (2¼ in.). Middle Amazon. Sex differences: male slenderer and more brightly coloured than female. A peaceful species which can be kept in all types of water. As a typical rain-forest fish it can only be bred in soft, rain-forest type water. Fish aged 1–2 years are best for breeding purposes. Rearing is not always easy and should be done in a spacious tank. A very prolific species, but like others in this genus it is very prone to eating its own eggs. May be attacked by neon disease. *Hemigrammus pulcher* is more warmth-loving than most species in the genus *Hemigrammus* and for breeding the water temperature should be 25–27°C (77–81°F).

32. *Petitella georgiae*
[*Hemigrammus rhodostomus*]
Red-nosed Tetra
4·5 cm (1¾ in.). Lower Amazon. Sex differences: male slenderer and rather more brightly coloured than female.

Care and breeding as for the preceding species, but rearing presents even more difficulties.

33. *Hemigrammus unilineatus*
One-line Tetra

5 cm (2 in.). Northern South America and Trinidad. Sex difference: male usually somewhat slenderer than female. Care and breeding as for No. 12.

34. *Hyphessobrycon bifasciatus*
Yellow Tetra

5 cm (2 in.). South-east Brazil, near the coast. Sex differences: male slenderer than female, with whitish-blue front edges to the dorsal and anal fins. An undemanding shoaling fish which does well in all types of water. It often spawns in groups and the slightly adhesive eggs (up to 300) are laid in among or close to fine-leaved plants. Temperature 22–25° (72–77°F). The young are tiny, and during the first week they should be fed on *Paramecium, Cyclops* nauplii and rotifers. Growth is very rapid.

35. *Hyphessobrycon serpae*
[*Hyphessobrycon callistus serpae*]

4·5 cm (1¾ in.). Middle Amazon to Paraguay. Sex differences: male slenderer and a brighter red than female. This form (as *H. callistus serpae*) and *H. c. bentosi, H. c. callistus, H. c. copelandi, H. c. minor* and *H. c. rosaceus* have all been considered to be subspecies of *Hyphessobrycon callistus*. The species occurs in colour varieties, with and without the shoulder marking and in various shades of red.

This fish can be regarded as the prototype for a large number of the species that follow, insofar as general care and breeding are concerned. Like most other rain-forest fishes it thrives in both soft and hard water at pH

6–7 and a temperature of 23–26°C (73–79°F). It prefers live food but will also do well on dead food, such as fish flesh, cod or other roe and on the various dried foods on the market as well as on trout food. For breeding one should use an all-glass tank or a glass one glued together with silicone cement. After being thoroughly cleaned this should be filled with soft water: rain water, demineralised water or natural water which has been filtered through sphagnum moss for 8–14 days. The bottom should be covered with a large amount of coarse sphagnum (2–3 cm, *c.* 1 in. thick) or with some form of mesh or grating. The latter can be a piece of black or dark green nylon net (mesh size 5–6 mm, *c.* ⅕ in.) spread out 3–4 cm (*c.* 1½ in.) above the bottom. For spawning cover it is best to use fine-leaved plants, such as Java Moss, which will tolerate dim light and acid water; the artificial green nylon algae can also be used. For forms which spawn near the surface the floating fern *Ceratopteris* is very suitable. The tank should be positioned in a place with subdued light. When the breeding tank has been set up and the temperature is at 25–27°C (77–81°F), it should be allowed to stand for about 14 days before the breeding fish are put in. The capacity of the tank depends upon the size of the species and its productivity, but a tank holding 30–50 litres (8–13¼ U.S. gals) is usually best.

For breeding stock the fish should be young and preferably under 2 years old. They should be introduced to the breeding tank in the evening and if they have not spawned after 3 days they should be taken out again. They should not be fed while in the breeding tank. The eggs usually hatch in 24–48 hours and the larvae hang from the plants for a further 5 days before they are free-swimming and feeding can begin. Young of almost all the random-spawning rain-forest characins are small and stationary. They should therefore be fed on very tiny live food such as *Paramecium, Cyclops* and *Diaptomus* nauplii or on rotifers. After the first 8 days the water should be gently aerated and after 14 days one can start to change about a quarter of the water every fortnight; the new water should be ordinary fresh, hard tap water. After 14 days the young can be fed on *Artemia* nauplii. As they grow, and depending upon the size of the brood, they should be transferred to a larger tank. When they are about a month old most of them will start to take sieved *Cyclops*, small *Daphnia* and fine dried food. They should be fed at least twice a day but only with as much as they will eat in 3–4 hours.

36. *Hyphessobrycon flammeus*
Flame Tetra

4·5 cm (1¾ in.). The area of Rio de Janeiro. Sex differences: male slenderer than female and with a dark edge to the anal fin. Also in the male the pelvic and anal fins are a brighter red than in the female. A hardy shoaling fish which breeds readily. It can be bred as described under No. 35, but will also breed in any kind of ordinary tap water. The brood may have up to 300 eggs.

37. *Hyphessobrycon georgettae*

Male 2·5 cm (1 in.), female 3·5 cm (1½ in.). River Sipalwini in southern Surinam. Sex differences: the male is slenderer and a more intense pink than the female and his dorsal fin has a larger dark marking. Care and breeding as for No. 35. Brood 50–80. A species that is seldom seen.

38. *Hyphessobrycon griemi*
Griem's Tetra

4·5 cm (1¾ in.). Many localities in Brazil. Sex differences: male slenderer and more brightly coloured than female. This species is probably closely related to No. 36, and should be kept and bred in the same way.

39. *Hyphessobrycon heterorhabdus*
Flag Tetra

5 cm (2 in.). Lower Amazon, Rio Tocantins. Sex difference: when seen in transmitted light the rear of the male's body cavity is pointed, whereas in the female it is rounded. An attractive but delicate little fish. Care and breeding as for No. 35. Often attacked by neon disease.

40. *Hyphessobrycon herbertaxelrodi*
Black Neon

4·5 cm (1¾ in.). Brazil, the state of Mato Grosso, Rio Taquari. Sex differences: male somewhat smaller and slenderer than female. Care and breeding as for No. 35. Brood up to 180.

41. *Hyphessobrycon ornatus*

5 cm (2 in.). Lower Amazon. Sex differences: see the illustration. A very attractive and hardy shoaling fish which should be kept and bred as described for No. 35. Brood up to 300.

42. *Hyphessobrycon heterorhabdus*
[*Hyphessobrycon peruvianus*]

4 cm (1½ in.). Iquitos in the Peruvian part of the Amazon. Sex differences: male slenderer with more intense colours than female. Care and breeding as for No. 35.

43. *Hyphessobrycon pulchripinnis*
Lemon Tetra

5 cm (2 in.). Large areas of the

Amazon. Sex differences: male slenderer, his anal fin with a black edge lacking in the female. Care and breeding as for No. 35. Brood up to 300.

44. Hyphessobrycon 'roberti'
6 cm (2¼ in.). Exact distribution not known. Sex difference: dorsal and anal fins more elongated in male than in female. This form is probably closely related to the true *Hyphessobrycon rosaceus*. Care and breeding as for No. 35.

45. Hyphessobrycon rubrostigma
Bleeding Heart Tetra
8 cm (3 in.). The sources of the Amazon in Columbia. Sex differences: male's dorsal fin much elongated. Male's 'heart' marking often a more intense red than the female's. This very attractive tetra should be kept in a rain-forest tank with a capacity of over 100 litres (26½ U.S. gals) and preferably in a shoal of at least ten. It will appreciate some insect food, such as fruit-flies. This species has a tendency to become shy when kept in small or sparsely planted tanks.

46. Hyphessobrycon scholzei
Black-line Tetra
5 cm (2 in.). In the region of Pará. Sex differences: male slenderer with darker markings. A hardy shoaling species which should be kept and bred like No. 35, but it will breed in any type of water.

47. Cheirodon simulans
[Hyphessobrycon simulans]
Male 4 cm (1½ in.), female 5 cm (2 in.). Probably from the Rio Iufaris, a tributary of the Rio Negro, but the distribution is not fully known. Sex differences: male slenderer and more brightly coloured than female. It has been suggested that this is a variety of No. 51, but on the basis of its behaviour and its chromosome composition it must be regarded as a separate species. It is essentially a shoaling fish which keeps to the upper water layers. It can be kept and bred like No. 35, but breeding is difficult, so the species is not widely distributed in the aquarium world. It has a tendency to stop growing when subjected to irregular feeding.

48. Hyphessobrycon heterorhabdus
[Hyphessobrycon stegemanni]
4 cm (1½ in.). Streams in the savanna region between the lower Rio Tocantins and Rio Capim in north-eastern Brazil. Care and breeding as for No. 35.

49. Hyphessobrycon takasei
3·5 cm (1¼ in.). Northern Brazil. Sex difference: male slenderer than female. This species has not been bred in captivity but it should probably be treated like No. 35.

50. Hyphessobrycon vilmae
4 cm (1½ in.). Savanna areas near the Rio Arinos. Sex differences: male slenderer than female, and with whiter fin tips. Care and breeding as for No. 35. There are only scattered observations on the breeding of this tetra.

51. Cheirodon axelrodi
Cardinal Tetra
5 cm (2 in.). Rio Negro. Sex differences: female stouter and a little paler than male. This species aroused great interest on account of its fantastic colours when introduced to the aquarium world in 1956. It is a hardy fish and should be kept like the other tetras. For most aquarists, however, it is not easy to breed. Among European breeders there is a certain amount of disagreement concerning the general conditions and water type.

Most of the successful breeding appears to be from imported fish or from young first generation breeding stock. Certain authors consider that it is the males, in particular, which lose fertility in the course of a few generations. It has also been said that large commercial breeders purposely sterilise the fish. In general, the conditions should probably be as given under No. 35, with the temperature at 25–27°C (77–81°F). The brood varies considerably in size (50–200) and the young grow slowly and are at first stationary, like other rain-forest tetras.

52. *Paracheirodon innesi*
Neon Tetra
4 cm (1½ in.). Upper Amazon (Leticia-Tabatinga region). Sex differences: male slenderer with the red stripe brighter in colour and more pointed at the front. On account of its extraordinary beauty and hardiness this species has gained great favour with aquarists. It should be kept and bred like No. 35, except that it does best at a temperature of 20–23°C (68–73°F). It should never be kept above 24°C (75°F). For breeding it is best to use 1–2-year-old fish. They usually spawn in groups, the eggs being laid in among fine-leaved plants. It is important to acclimatise the young to hard water, as they are particularly susceptible to the dreaded neon disease when kept in rain-forest water. This disease can be detected in many stocks by the appearance of pale areas on the body. Brood 50–200.

53. *Ladigesia roloffi*
3 cm (1¼ in.). Liberia. Sex differences: male slenderer with brighter red on the fins than the female. A very delicate species which should be kept as a shoal and not together with larger species. Breeding as for No. 35. The young are very tiny. The female lays eggs in the lower water layers, just above the bottom. This species likes a densely planted aquarium.

54. *Megalamphodus megalopterus*
4·5 cm (1¾ in.). Brazil, Mato Grosso. Sex differences: the illustration shows a male; the female is smaller with a red ground colour and red fins. Care and breeding as for No. 35.

55. *Megalamphodus sweglesi*
4 cm (1½ in.). Colombia, Upper Amazon. Sex differences: male slenderer than female, with a pointed, elongated dorsal fin. Care and breeding as for No. 35. This species is very difficult to breed and many of the young die.

56. *Phenacogrammus interruptus*
[*Micralestes interruptus*]
Congo Tetra
Male 8 cm (3 in.), female 7 cm (2¾ in.). Zaïre region. Sex differences: see illustration. A very attractive species which should be kept in a large tank with plenty of open space for swimming. Temperature: 25–27°C (77–81°F). Thrives in all types of water. Omnivorous, but is particularly fond of insects which it snaps up at the surface. Spawning takes place near the bottom. After preliminary chasing by the male, he comes to rest, with fins quivering, just above the bottom, the ripe female approaches from the side and mating takes place as the male curls his anal fin over the tail region of the female. At each of these matings the female lays 6–8 very large, yellowish eggs. The period of spawning extends over several days. Unfortunately few of the eggs hatch. This species requires soft, slightly acid water. The females are bad egg-eaters. The young are not difficult to rear, see No. 35.

57. *Alestopetersius caudalis*
Yellow Congo Characin
7 cm (2¾ in.). Lower Zaïre and its tributaries. Sex differences: in the male the dorsal fin has very elongated rays which are usually black towards the tip; the anal and pelvic fins also have elongated rays in the male, and the central rays of the caudal fin are elongated and jet-black. Care and breeding as for No. 56.

58. *Boehlkea fredcochui*
   [*Microbrycon cochui*]
3·5 cm (1¼ in.). Upper Amazon in the region of Ramon Castillo. Sex differences: male slenderer than female and with a more prominent dark, lateral stripe. Care and breeding as for No. 22, but in this species the young are very tiny and can only take the finest forms of live food.

59. *Moenkhausia oligolepis*
Glass Tetra
12 cm (4¾ in.). Amazon and Guyana. Sex differences: male smaller and slenderer than female. Care and breeding as for No. 20.

60. *Moenkhausia pittieri*
6 cm (2¼ in.). Venezuela. Sex difference: dorsal fin larger in the male than the female. Care and breeding as for No. 35, but *Moenkhausia pittieri* can also be bred in hard water. Spawning is often violent. Some of the young can be reared in a community tank.

61. *Moenkhausia sanctaefilomenae*
   [*Moenkhausia sanctae-filomenae*]
7 cm (2¾ in.). Rivers in Paraguay and in the Paranaiba basin. Sex difference: male slenderer than female. Care and breeding as for No. 20.

62. *Nematobrycon palmeri*
6 cm (2¼ in.). Care and breeding as for No. 35. Old males may be very aggressive towards other members of their own species. The female does not lay a particularly large number of eggs. This species becomes increasingly stationary with age.

63. *Nematobrycon lacortei*
   [*Nematobrycon amphiloxus*]
6 cm (2¼ in.). Western Colombia, Rio Atrato. This species was imported into the United States, a few years ago but it is not as attractively coloured as *Nematobrycon palmeri*. Care and breeding as for No. 35. The males may be very aggressive.

64. *Pristella riddlei*
X-ray Fish
4·5 cm (1¾ in.). Venezuela, Guyana and Lower Amazon. Sex differences: male slenderer and more brightly coloured than female. An attractive little fish which thrives in all types of water. It can be bred like No. 35, but also in medium-hard water with a little added salt. Brood up to 300. The adults are notorious egg-eaters.

65. *Pseudocorynopoma doriae*
Dragon-finned Characin
8 cm (3 in.). Brazil and La Plata. Sex difference: the unpaired fins of the male are much elongated. A hardy species which does best in hard water at 18–23°C (64–73°F). Breeding and behaviour as for No. 18.

Lebiasinidae U.S.A.
Characidae Britain

66. *Pyrrhulina vittata*
Striped Vittata
7 cm (1¾ in.). Amazon at Santarem, Rio Tapajoz. Sex differences: adult males have yellowish or red fins and the upper lobe of the caudal fin is somewhat elongated. This species practises brood protection. The eggs are laid on the upperside of leaves, and are not very adhesive. The male

uses his pectoral and ventral fins to fan fresh water over the eggs. Brood up to 100. The young can be reared as for No. 16.

Characidae

67. Thayeria boehlkei
7 cm (2¾ in.). Upper Amazon. Sex difference: the ripe females are stouter at spawning time. A hardy species which will do well in any type of water. For breeding the tank should have a capacity of c. 100 litres (26½ U.S. gals), as spawning may be very violent and the females may be damaged by the males. A single female may lay over 1,000 eggs, but the majority of these do not develop so there is a danger that micro-organisms may proliferate and then attack the viable, fertilised eggs. This is another reason for using a large tank for breeding. This species should be bred at a temperature of 26–28°C (79–82°F) in slightly acid water (DH below 8°). The young are very small and for the first week should be fed on tiny live food. This species has been erroneously known as *Thayeria obliqua*.

68. Thayeria ifati
7 cm (2¾ in.). Lower Amazon. Otherwise as for No. 67.

69. Thayeria obliqua
    Penguin Fish
7 cm (2¾ in.). Lower Amazon. Otherwise as for No. 67.

70. Thayeria sanctaemariae
    [*Thayeria sanctae-mariae*]
7 cm (2¾ in.). Lower Amazon. Otherwise as for No. 67.

Anostomidae

A South American family of which only a few species are common as aquarium fishes. Most of them have a cigar-shaped body and a small mouth. In the wild these fishes usually live in small shoals in slow-flowing waters. Many of the species take up an oblique position with the head down, both when swimming and when stationary. All the forms described here are rain-forest fishes which should not be kept at temperatures below 24°C (75°F). Most are omnivorous, but are particularly fond of worms. Only a few species have been bred in captivity.

71. Abramites microcephalus
    Headstander
13 cm (5 in.). Lower Amazon. Sex differences: none have been described. A peaceful fish which should be kept in a large tank. Breeding in the aquarium has not been described.

72. Anostomus anostomus
    Striped Anostomus
14 cm (5½ in.). Guyana, southwards to Manaos. Sex differences: not known with any certainty, but the male may be slenderer than the female. This is the commonest species in the genus *Anostomus* but it has not bred in the aquarium.

Chilodontidae U.S.A.
Anostomidae Britain

73. Chilodus punctatus
    Spotted Headstander
7 cm (2¾ in.). Large areas of northern South America, Orinoco, Rio Negro and the central Amazon region. Sex difference: only apparent in fish ready to spawn, when the female's belly is more rounded. It has not been confirmed that the dorsal fin is taller in the male than in the female. This species should be kept as described under the family Anostomidae. It is important to give breeding stock a varied diet of gnat or mosquito

larvae, *Tubifex* and Grindal worms, as well as a vegetable supplement in the form of algae or soft water-plants. The water should be free of impurities, with a hardness of less than 10° DH, and slightly acid (filter through sphagnum moss). The breeding tank should have a capacity of at least 80 litres (21 U.S. gals). Java moss is suitable as a spawning plant. The breeding tank should be in a quiet position and slightly shaded, and kept at a temperature of *c.* 26°C (79°F). Spawning is usually not violent, and 3–5 eggs, each *c.* 1·5 mm in diameter, are laid at each mating. These hatch in 30–36 hours and the young are free-swimming after a further 5 days. They can be fed immediately on *Artemia* nauplii and they grow rapidly, but are sensitive to changes in the composition of the water. Acclimatisation to hard water is therefore a slow process.

Lebiasinidae U.S.A.
Hemiodontidae Britain
A South American family which is similar to the Anostomidae in form and habits. The species of the genus *Nannostomus* are particularly popular in the aquarium. They are all small and can be kept and bred like No. 35. The family name refers to the fact that in most of the species there are no teeth in the lower jaw. It is a characteristic of the *Nannostomus* species that at night they assume a special pattern which is completely different from the daytime pattern. An adipose fin is present in some species, absent in others (see the illustrations).

74. *Nannostomus beckfordi*
[*Nannostomus beckfordi anomalus*]
Golden Pencilfish
4·5 cm (1¾ in.). Guyana, Paraná, Rio Negro, and middle and lower Amazon. Sex difference: male slenderer than female. The anal fin and the lower lobe of the caudal fin are red in the male, colourless in the female. Breeding as for No. 35. Brood up to 200 eggs. The adults are inveterate egg-eaters.

75. *Nannostomus beckfordi*
[*Nannostomus beckfordi aripirangensis*]
Golden Pencilfish
4 cm (1½ in.). Aripiranga Island in the Lower Amazon. Sex differences: the illustration shows a male; the female lacks the male's bright red colour and the pale blue tips to the pectoral fins and she is stouter. Breeding as for No. 35. Brood up to 200; the parents are bad egg-eaters.

76. *Nannostomus bifasciatus*
Two-banded Pencilfish
6 cm (2¼ in.). Surinam. Sex differences: male slenderer and with more red on the caudal fin. This species should be treated like the preceding two forms, to which it is closely related.

77. *Nannostomus espei*
4 cm (1½ in.). Exact distribution not known. Sex differences: the long lateral golden stripes are more prominent and the front rays of the anal fin are darker in the male than in the female; the male is also somewhat slenderer. Care and breeding as for the other members of the genus, but there are few records of successful breeding.

78. *Poecilobrycon eques*
[*Nannostomus eques*]
Tube-mouthed Pencilfish
5 cm (2 in.). Middle Amazon region. Sex differences: male slenderer than female, and with a red marking on the anal fin which is normally lacking in the female. This species usually lives in the upper layers, its body held

obliquely, with the head up. It should be kept and bred like the other species in the genus. The species is not particularly prolific, and there are seldom more than 50–60 young in a brood.

79. *Poecilobrycon harrisoni*
     [*Nannostomus harrisoni*]
6 cm (2¼ in.). Western Guyana, near Christiansburg. Sex difference: only apparent in sexually mature fish, when the female is slightly stouter than the male. This species is difficult to breed as the females rarely succeed in producing eggs in the aquarium.

80. *Nannostomus marginatus*
     marginatus
     Dwarf Pencilfish
4 cm (1½ in.). Surinam, western Guyana. Sex differences: male slenderer and with more red on the fins than the female. In most of the males the rear edge of the anal fin has a black border which is usually lacking in the females. An attractive but not very prolific species which seldom produces broods of more than 30. The adults are bad egg-eaters, so the tank should be densely planted and possibly also fitted with some form of breeding trap.

81. *Nannostomus marginatus*
     picturatus
Differs only in appearance from No. 80.

82. *Nannostomus trifasciatus*
     Three-banded Pencilfish
6 cm (2¼ in.). Central Amazon, western Guyana, Rio Negro. Sex differences: only apparent in fish ready to spawn, when the male is slightly slenderer than the female. When seen in transmitted light one can discern the eggs in ripe females, just in front of the anus. This very attractive species should be kept like

the others in the genus, but it is certainly the most difficult to breed. In fact this has only been successful with imported specimens. The males indulge in ritual fighting, in which they slap one another with their tails. Spawning often takes place among the roots of floating plants. The brood is quite small.

83. *Poecilobrycon unifasciatus*
     [*Nannostomus unifasciatus*]
     One-lined Pencilfish
6·5 cm (2½ in.). Middle and lower Amazon, Rio Negro. Sex difference: the margin of the anal fin is rounded in the male, straight in the female. This is another species which is very difficult to breed.

Citharinidae
A family with representatives in many parts of Africa, but with only a few species small enough to be suitable for the home aquarium.

84. *Neolebias ansorgii*
     [*Neolebias ansorgei*]
3·5 cm (1½ in.). Sex difference: belly profile more convex in female than in male. A rather shy species which only thrives in a tank with densely planted vegetation. Many authors recommend that a single pair should be kept in a small tank. These fish require pure, clear water and should be fed on live food, such as small *Daphnia, Cyclops* and Grindal worms. For breeding it is best to use a small all-glass tank with clear, slightly acid water, hardness 5–10° DH. The substrate can be sphagnum moss. Java moss or the fern *Ceratopteris* are suitable as spawning plants. It is quite usual for spawning, which takes place among the plants, to extend over a period of 2–3 days. At each pairing the female lays 5–10 eggs, and the total for a single spawning period may be

100–200. The fry, which are small, should be treated as for No. 35.

85. *Neolebias unifasciatus*
4·5 cm (1¾ in.). Tropical West Africa. For sex differences, care and breeding, see the preceding species.

86. *Nannaethiops unitaeniatus*
One-striped African Characin
6·5 cm (2½ in.). Widely distributed in central Africa. Sex differences: female paler than male; during spawning the front part of the dorsal fin and the upper caudal fin lobe of the male are blood-red. Care and breeding as for No. 12.

Gasteropelecidae
Hatchetfishes
A South American family in which the species have a tall laterally compressed body, with a much protruding breast region. This is due to the enlargement of the shoulder girdle which supplies attachment for the powerful muscles of the pectoral fins. By beating these fins and also the tail these fishes are capable of propelling themselves out of the water and gliding over the surface for distances of 3–5 metres (10–16 feet). Hatchetfishes are typical surface-living forms (with a straight dorsal profile) and most of the species are fairly stationary. They should be treated as rainforest fishes. The most natural food would be small insects, such as fruitflies, which they snap up at the surface, but they can also be accustomed to taking ordinary live food.

Little is known about their breeding, and the few published accounts are rather contradictory.

87. *Carnegiella marthae*
Black-winged Hatchetfish
3·5 cm (1½ in.). Venezuela, Peru, Rio Negro and Orinoco. Sex differences:

not known. For care, see the family description.

88. *Carnegiella myersi*
3 cm (1¼ in.). Peru, upper Amazon and tributaries of the Marañon. A very delicate little fish which has never been widely distributed in the aquarium world. For care, see the family description.

89. *Carnegiella strigata strigata*
Marbled Hatchetfish
4·5 cm (1¾ in.). Small pools in the Amazon region. Sex differences: none described. For care, see the family description. According to one author this species spawns among the stems of *Myriophyllum*.

90. *Carnegiella strigata vesca*
Western Guyana and lower Amazon. Care, as for family.

91. *Gasteropelecus sternicla*
Common Hatchetfish
6·5 cm (2½ in.). Amazon basin and Guyana. Sex differences: not described. This species should be kept in a tank holding more than 100 litres (26½ U.S. gals) of water.

92. *Thoracocharax stellatus*
7 cm (2¾ in.). Widely distributed in Brazil. Sex differences: not described. Care, as for the family.

Cyprinidae
Carps and barbs
A very large family with species that live under a wide range of environmental conditions and show a great variety of adaptations. There are about 1500 different species in the family, and some such as those in the genera *Barbus, Danio* and *Rasbora* are really classical aquarium fishes. All the species lack an adipose fin and jaw teeth and many have two or four barbels.

93. *Barbus arulius*

10–12 cm (3¾–4¾ in.). South-eastern India, Travancore, Cauvery. Sex differences: in adult males, but not in females, the dorsal fin rays are much elongated; the male is also slenderer than the female. This is an attractive species which should be kept in a tank with a capacity of over 250 litres (66 U.S. gals). Like most of the barbs it thrives best in hard water, with a quarter of the volume being regularly replaced with fresh tap water. Temperature: 24–25°C (75–77°F). The tank should be densely planted with species of *Cryptocoryne* and fine-leaved plants. Most barbs like to have the water kept moving. They can be fed on all kinds of live food, but the majority will do very well on dried food, provided they are also given a certain amount of vegetable matter. They are all peaceful, shoaling fishes, which can be kept together with other species of the same genus.

Most of the barbs can be bred in medium-hard (7–10° DH), neutral water. Fine-leaved plants, such as *Myriophyllum, Cabomba* or Java moss are suitable for spawning which often takes place in the early hours of the morning; a little sunlight evidently stimulates spawning. The male usually chases the female very actively, but this does not always happen. The actual pairing normally takes place among plant stems, the partners pressing against one another, and quivering as they release eggs and sperms, often in large quantities. The fertilised eggs sink to the bottom or adhere to the plants. They hatch in 24–36 hours and the young are free-swimming after a further 3–4 days. The young, which are not difficult to rear, can be fed at first on *Paramecium* and after 2–3 days on *Artemia* nauplii or micro-worms. Growth is rapid, and about one quarter of the water should be changed every week. When the young are about 1 cm (⅓ in.) long they can be given a dried food containing some vegetable matter.

For *Barbus arulius* the breeding tank should have a capacity of over 80 litres (21 U.S. gals(. In spite of its size this is not a particularly prolific species.

94. *Barbus conchonius*
Rosy Barb

Up to 14 cm (5½ in.). Bengal, Assam and northern India, in running waters. Sex differences: the illustration shows a male in breeding dress; the female is paler with colourless fins. A very hardy barb which thrives at a temperature of 18–25°C (64–77°F). Care and breeding as for No. 93; this is a very prolific species which will breed successfully in a tank holding 30–50 litres (8–13¼ U.S. gals).

95. *Barbus gelius*
Golden Dwarf Barb

4 cm (1½ in.). Bengal and central India. Sex difference: ripe females are stouter than males. An undemanding species which should always be kept in a small shoal. Temperature: 19–22°C (66–72°F). These fish will breed in a small tank 15–20 litres (4–5¼ U.S. gals). Otherwise as for No. 93.

96. *Barbus hulstaerti*

3 cm (1¼ in.). Lower Zaïre. Sex differences: male larger, with black and bright yellow and red on the fins; the female's fins are paler. This very attractive species is not easy to keep but it seems to do best in medium-hard or hard water, kept slightly moving; a proportion of the water should be changed regularly. This species should be kept on its own in a small tank. It is omnivorous,

but will only take small food. It has not been regularly bred in the aquarium. Temperature: 24–27°C (75–81°F).

97. *Barbus nigrofasciatus*
Black Ruby

6 cm (2¼ in.). Southern Sri Lanka (formerly Ceylon), in slow-flowing or standing waters in the lowlands. Sex differences: the illustration shows a male in breeding dress; the female has colourless fins and 3–4 indistinct greyish transverse bands. Apart from these points the sexes can be distinguished by the appearance of the dorsal fins which are black in the male, colourless in the female. This popular species should be kept and bred like No. 93. For breeding the temperature should be 27°C (81°F). Brood up to 300.

98. *Barbus oligolepis*
Island Barb

5 cm (2 in.). Sumatra. Sex differences: in the male the dorsal and anal fins have a black border and the fins are, in general, more orange or brick-red. The females lack the black fin edges and their general coloration is duller. Care and breeding as for No. 93. This lively barb can be bred in a small tank.

99. *Barbus pentazona pentazona*
Five-banded Barb

5 cm (2 in.). Malaya, Singapore, Borneo and Sumatra. Sex differences: male a brighter red than the female, which is duller and stouter. For breeding, which is not easy, this species requires soft, slightly acid water.

100. *Barbus 'schuberti'*
Golden Barb

A mutation or 'sport' of another species of *Barbus*, perhaps No. 101.

101. *Barbus semifasciolatus*
Green Barb

7 cm (2¾ in.). South-east China. Sex differences: male slenderer than female, and at spawning time the male's belly is red. Care and breeding as for No. 93.

102. *Barbus stoliczkanus*
Stoliczka's Barb

6 cm (2¼ in.). Burma, in the lower Irrawaddy. Sex differences: male slenderer than female and on the dorsal fin a red and black pattern, which the female lacks. Care and breeding as for No. 93.

103. *Barbus tetrazona tetrazona*
Tiger Barb

6 cm (2¼ in.). Sex differences: male slenderer than female. The fins of the male are reddish, whereas those of the female are more orange-yellow. A very popular species which has been bred for many years. This has resulted, among other things, in an irregular distribution of black pigment on the body of some individuals. For breeding purposes it is, therefore, essential only to use regularly striped individuals. The breeding tank should have a capacity of 25–40 litres (6½–10½ U.S. gals), and fish 1–2 years old are the most suitable. When spawning the male curls his tail around the rear half of the female, from above. A very prolific species.

104. *Barbus titteya*
Cherry Barb

5 cm (2 in.). Sri Lanka, in streams. Sex differences: fins and body brilliant red in the male, paler and more ochre-coloured in the female. Care and breeding as for No. 93.

105. *Brachydanio albolineatus*
Pearl Danio

5·5 cm (2⅛ in.). Sumatra and South-east Asia. Sex differences: male slenderer and more intensely coloured than female. A very lively, omnivorous shoaling fish which does best in hard water at a temperature of 22–25°C (72–77°F). Breeding, as for No. 12.

106. *Brachydanio frankei*
4·5 cm (1¾ in.). Southern Asia. This species should be kept like No. 105.

107. *Brachydanio nigrofasciatus*
Spotted Danio
4 cm (1½ in.). Burma. Sex differences, care and breeding as for No. 105, but somewhat more difficult to breed and less prolific than the other species in the genus.

108. *Brachydanio rerio*
Zebra Danio
4·5 cm (1¾ in.). Eastern India. Sex differences, care and breeding as for No. 105. One of the easiest egg-laying species to breed.

109. *Labeo bicolor*
Red-tailed Black 'Shark'
15 cm (6 in.). Thailand. A very attractive fish which thrives best in a large tank with patches of dense vegetation and numerous hiding-places. It is omnivorous but should be given a certain amount of vegetable matter. Adult specimens are very territorial and may be extremely aggressive towards other members of their own species. There are only a few accounts of breeding, which takes place in water with a hardness of 6·4–14° DH and a pH of 6·6–7·0. The eggs are laid in holes or crevices and it has been reported that they are guarded by the male. The young can at first be fed on powdered food, and later on *Artemia* nauplii. There are evidently no accounts of breeding in Europe or the United States.

110. *Labeo erythrurus*
12 cm (4¾ in.). Thailand, in the River Mekong near Kemarat. Care as for No. 109.

111. *Tanichthys albonubes*
White Cloud Mountain
Minnow
4 cm (1½ in.). China, Canton and Hongkong. Sex differences: male slenderer and more brightly coloured than female. This species should be kept in a small tank at ordinary room temperatures (18–21°C, 64–70°F). It does best in hard, neutral water, in a tank with fine-leaved plants. Spawning takes place over a period of several days and, if well fed, the adults do not attack their offspring which can be reared in the same tank, and fed in the same way as those of No. 93. This species becomes somewhat stationary and pale as it grows old.

112. *Rasbora borapetensis*
5 cm (2 in.). Thailand. Sex difference: male slenderer than female. Care and breeding as for No. 93.

113. *Rasbora hengeli*
4 cm (1½ in.). Sumatra. Sex difference: male slenderer than female. Care and breeding as for No. 35. The eggs are laid on leaves of *Cryptocoryne*, usually on the underside. The ripe female places her belly against the underside of the leaf, the male swims up alongside her and curves his tail around her back. At each such pairing the female lays 5–10 eggs which are immediately fertilised by the male. The eggs may also be laid on strips of green plastic. About 150 eggs in a brood.

114. *Rasbora heteromorpha*
Harlequin Fish
4·5 cm (1¾ in.). Malaya, Thailand and eastern Sumatra. Sex difference: the

lower front corner of the wedge-shaped marking is more pointed and produced in the male than in the female. Breeding as for No. 113, except that the Harlequin is more prolific, the females producing broods of up to 250 eggs. As in No. 113 the eggs are laid on broad leaves of water plants such as *Cryptocoryne*. The young can be reared like those of No. 93.

115. *Rasbora maculata*
Spotted Rasbora

2·5 cm (1 in.). Malaya and Sumatra. Sex differences: male slenderer and more brightly coloured than the female. On account of its size this species should be kept by itself in a small tank or together with Nos. 117 and 119. It can be bred in a very small tank like No. 35. Spawning takes place either in open water near the bottom or close to vegetation. The broods are not large (20–40 eggs). The young can be reared like those of No. 93, and they grow rapidly.

116. *Rasbora pauciperforata*
Red-striped Rasbora

7 cm (2¾ in.). Sumatra. Sex differences: male slenderer and a little smaller than female. Care and breeding as for No. 93.

117. *Rasbora somphongsi*

Male 3 cm (1¼ in.), female 3·5 cm (1⅜ in.). Thailand, in tributaries of the Menam. Breeding biology as for Nos. 113 and 114. General care and rearing of the young as for No. 93. The broods contain about 100 eggs.

118. *Rasbora trilineata*
Scissortail

Up to 15 cm (6 in.), but seldom more than 8 cm (3 in.) in the aquarium.

Malaya and the Greater Sunda Islands. Sex difference: male slenderer than female. This species should be kept as a shoal in a large aquarium tank and cared for as No. 93.

119. *Rasbora urophthalma*

2·5 cm (1 in.). Sumatra. Sex differences: male slenderer and a little smaller than female. During spawning the male's longitudinal stripe appears golden. Care and breeding as for No. 115.

120. *Rasbora vaterifloris*
Pearly Rasbora

4 cm (1½ in.). Sri Lanka, in mountain streams. Sex differences: male slenderer and with longer fins than the female. This species is sometimes difficult to acclimatise and is susceptible to disease. The water must be kept moving. Although omnivorous, part of its diet should consist of insects; in the wild it is said to feed largely on ants. This species requires slightly acid water for spawning, and the tank must be scrupulously cleaned and preferably have no plants.

Gyrinocheilidae

This family, which may in the future be merged with the Cyprinidae, contains only three species. All belong to the genus *Gyrinocheilus*, and all are from south-east Asia.

121. *Gyrinocheilus aymonieri*

Up to 30 cm (12 in.), but considerably less in the aquarium. Thailand, in running water. Sex differences: not known. This species should be kept in a large tank with clean water, but it does not require any special type of water. Large specimens may be very aggressive towards one another. There are no records of breeding in captivity. This fish is an excellent consumer of algae in aquarium tanks.

Cobitidae
Loaches
The loaches are distributed throughout the Old World. They are typical bottom-living fishes with a straight belly profile and a variable number of barbels. Just below the eye they have a spine which is directed backwards, but can be erected at right angles to the head. It then serves as a defence weapon against enemies. In many species there is a form of intestinal breathing. At intervals the fish takes in a mouthful of air which is passed backwards along the alimentary canal. The oxygen in the air is absorbed by the mucosa of the gut, particularly of the hind-gut. The remainder of the air is expelled through the anus. Intestinal respiration is an adaptation to the conditions in the stagnant, turbid, oxygen-deficient waters in which many of the species live. Most of the loaches are easy to keep. They do not require any special type of water, are omnivorous and the species described here all thrive at 24–27°C (75–81°F). Most of these species have not yet been bred in the aquarium.

122. *Acanthophthalmus cuneovirgatus*
5·5 cm (2¼ in.). Jahore. No external sex differences are known for the species of the genus *Acanthophthalmus*, which are known as Kuhlii Loaches. They should be kept without other fishes in a tank with pure, clear water and numerous hiding-places (crevices, roots, empty coconut shells). There are few detailed descriptions of breeding, but evidently this sometimes occurs when the fish are well fed but otherwise more or less left alone. Kuhlii Loaches are omnivorous and do best at 24–27°C

(75–81°F). They often reach a good age in the aquarium.

123. *Acanthophthalmus kuhlii kuhlii*
8 cm (3 in.). Java, Sumatra.

124. *Acanthophthalmus kuhlii sumatranus*
8 cm (3 in.). Sumatra.

125. *Acanthophthalmus myersi*
8 cm (3 in.). Thailand.

126. *Acanthophthalmus robiginosus*
[*Acanthophthalmus rubiginosus*]
5 cm (2 in.). Western Java.

127. *Acanthophthalmus semicinctus*
8 cm (3 in.). Sunda Islands. This is the commonest species on the market.

128. *Acanthophthalmus shelfordi*
8 cm (3 in.). Borneo.

129. *Botia macracantha*
Clown Loach
Up to 12 cm (4¾ in.). Sumatra, Borneo. Sex differences: not known. This species should be kept in a large tank with clear well-circulated water and patches of dense vegetation. It seems to thrive best in a shoal, but it is very susceptible to white spot (*Ichthyophthirius*) which may be difficult to cure with the usual drugs; Malachite Green has been used successfully. Not known to have bred in captivity.

130. *Botia modesta*
10 cm (3¾ in.). Malaya, Indonesia. Sex differences: not known. Care as for No. 129. Not yet bred in the aquarium.

131. *Botia sidthimunki*
6 cm (2¼ in.). Thailand. Sex differences: not known. Care as for No. 129. Only thrives when kept in a

173

group of ten or more. Not yet bred in the aquarium.

Catfishes
The catfishes of the suborder Siluroidea comprise over 2,000 species classified in about twenty different families. With the exception of those in the families Plotosidae (see page 233) and Ariidae, which live in brackish or salt waters, the catfishes are essentially fresh-water fishes, and most of them are bottom-living. All catfishes lack true scales, but certain families contain members with a different kind of bony armour.

Siluridae
This family of several genera is distributed in Europe and Asia. They are characterised by having 2–3 pairs of barbels and a completely naked skin (i.e. no armour); the dorsal fin is lacking or very small, the anal fin is very long, and the ventral fins are small or lacking.

132. *Kryptopterus bicirrhis*
Glass Catfish
9 cm (3½ in.). South-east Asia, Indonesia in running waters. Sex differences: not known. A catfish which should be kept in a large tank (over 200 litres, 53 U.S. gals) with good water circulation. It only thrives when kept as a small shoal, is not particular as regards the type of water, and feeds exclusively on small live food. The tank should not be too brightly lit. Temperature: 21–25°C (70–77°F). Not yet bred in the aquarium.

Schilbeidae
African and Asiatic catfishes that are very similar in form to the Siluridae.

133. *Etropiellus debauwi*
[*Etropiella debauwi*]
8 cm (3 in.). Zaïre, Stanley Pool. Sex

174

differences: not known. Care as for No. 132. A very lively fish which is constantly on the move.

Mochocidae
These fishes, which occur only in Africa, are not armoured. The dorsal and pectoral fins have powerful spines. All the species have an adipose fin, which is sometimes very large, and three pairs of barbels. These are crepuscular or nocturnal fishes which spend the day hidden beneath the river banks. In the aquarium they should be kept in dim light and given plenty of hiding-places. They are easy to keep but only a few have been known to breed, see No. 135.

134. *Synodontis angelicus*
20 cm (7¾ in.). Tropical West Africa, Zaïre. Sex differences: not described. The illustration shows a young specimen. When adult this species is greyish or dark violet with brownish markings. Not yet bred in captivity.

135. *Synodontis nigriventris*
Upside-down Catfish
9 cm (3½ in.). Central parts of the Zaïre basin. Sex differences: female larger and with fewer, larger dark spots on the body than the male. The latter also has a number of small dark spots on the back of the head, which are lacking in the female. The upside down swimming position is characteristic (see page 16). This species should be kept in a large tank with plenty of shelter. It thrives in all types of water, at a temperature of 24–27°C (75–81°F). Although omnivorous, these fish should be given a good supply of gnat or mosquito larvae if they are to develop eggs and sperms. A single case of breeding has been described. This took place in water with a hardness of 6° DH at 24–27°C

(75–81°F). The eggs were laid in clumps on the aquarium glass, in the darkest areas of the tank. They hatched in 7–8 days and the young had consumed the contents of their yolk sac after a further 4 days. They could then take *Artemia* nauplii. Growth was slow and the young began to swim upside down after 7–10 weeks.

Pimelodidae
A family with representatives in South and Central America, north to Mexico. These are elongated unarmoured fishes with three pairs of long barbels. Most species are small, but they are seldom imported. None have been bred in captivity and there are no known external differences between the sexes.

136. *Pimelodella picta*
    [*Pimelodella pictus*]
9 cm (3½ in.). Brazil, in running waters. A crespuscular and nocturnal species which should be kept in a dimly lit tank with plenty of hiding-places. Care as for No. 135.

Aspredinidae
These catfishes come from the western part of the Amazon region where they live in running water. They are active at night and spend the day buried in the bottom. They are very hardy, omnivorous fishes but because of their stationary and secretive habits they have never become very popular in the aquarium world. No external sex differences are known and none of the species have been bred.

137. *Bunocephalus kneri*
12 cm (4¾ in.). Western Amazon to Ecuador. They can be kept in any type of fresh water at a temperature of 21–25°C (70–77°F).

Loricariidae
Suckermouth Catfishes
These are typical bottom-living fishes from rivers in central and northern South America. The mouth is modified to form a suction organ surrounded by powerful lips. The two species described here have a heavy armour over the whole body, but in some other members of the family the ventral shields are lacking. The Suckermouth Catfishes are specialised for rasping algae and sessile invertebrates off rocks and roots. They have a special anatomical character, an iris-lobe. This is a small peg-shaped structure which extends down into the pupil; by expanding or contracting it regulates the amount of light entering the eye. When setting up the tank care should be taken to allow for a good circulation of the water. The temperature should be 21–24°C (70–75°F) but the actual type of water is not critical. They must be given a plentiful supply of plant food, and most species like to be able to hide among rocks and roots or to bury themselves in the bottom. Many species have bred in captivity, particularly those of *Loricaria* and *Otocinclus*.

138. *Loricaria parva*
12 cm (4¾ in.). Paraguay and La Plata. Sex differences: in the full-grown male the gill cover and the pectoral fins are covered with numerous bristles. These are lacking in the female which usually has a stouter belly than the male. The eggs are laid on a firm substrate in rock crevices or among roots and are said to be guarded by the male. They may also be laid in hollow branches, plastic tubes or dark glass tubing. Spawning usually takes place in the evening, particularly in December–February. During pairing the female attaches

herself firmly to one of the male's ventral fins. The eggs, of which there may be about 200, hatch in 8–9 days and the young are free-swimming 2 days later. They can be fed at first on micro-worms, but later they must have some vegetable matter.

Fish sold under the name *Loricaria parva* often belong to other species, including *L. filamentosa*.

139. Otocinclus affinis

4 cm (1½ in.). South-east Brazil in the region of Rio de Janeiro. Sex differences: female stouter than male. For care, see the family description. This species only thrives if given plenty of algae and other plant food. Spawning is similar to that of *Corydoras* species, see below. The eggs are small and laid on firm objects in the tank. They hatch in 2–3 days and the young can then be fed on micro-worms and later on *Artemia* nauplii and finely divided vegetable matter.

Callichthyidae
Armoured Catfishes

A large South American catfish family which contains several popular, small aquarium fishes. All the species have two rows of bony plates along the sides of the body. There is a large dorsal fin and a well-developed adipose fin. The mouth opens downwards and has one or two pairs of barbels. The eyes are movable. This family is distributed in running waters throughout South America and Trinidad. They often occur in large, mixed shoals, sometimes in muddy, oxygen-deficient water. Most of the species have alimentary respiration and are able to absorb oxygen from air bubbles that are swallowed and passed along the gut.

These are hardy, peaceful fishes which do best in large, shallow tanks

with patches of dense vegetation, neutral or slightly acid water and a certain amount of circulation. When searching for food they root about in the bottom, so this should not be too coarse or contain sharp stones. An efficient filter is necessary to remove suspended particles. It is a common mistake to think that the armoured catfishes can act as 'garbage collectors' and live off any surplus food left by other fishes, They do, in fact, require a rich and varied diet.

Only a few species have been regularly bred in the aquarium, namely *Corydoras aeneus, C. elegans* and *C. paleatus*. External sex differences are only apparent in adult specimens. The female is larger with a stouter belly, and the dorsal fin of the male is taller and more pointed than that of the female. It would not be possible to give any general advice on breeding, but certain things do appear to promote it: a large shallow tank with numerous hiding-places, a certain amount of sunlight and clear, neutral or slightly acid water that is free of bacteria. The water should be kept moving and have a hardness of 5–10° DH, and about one-third of it should be replaced every month. The diet should be plentiful with living (*Tubifex* and whiteworms) and dead animal and vegetable food. The water should not be too deep (20–30 cm, 8–12 in.) and the temperature should be around 25°C (77°F).

For breeding it is best to have a group of 2–3 females and double that number of males. Spawning starts when a couple of males pursue a female, which they touch with their barbels. After the female has swum around for a little time with the males dancing attendance, the fish start to clean various firm objects and leaves. Pairing takes place when a male uses his pectoral fins to grip the female's barbels and hold her against his belly; at the same time he releases a portion of sperms and the female lays 3–6 eggs which she holds in her ventral fins. At this point the male releases the female and she swims on through the cloud of sperms which fertilise the eggs she is carrying. After this she deposits the sticky eggs on firm objects which need not necessarily have been cleaned beforehand. This process is repeated several times within the same spawning period, and then another period may start after about a week.

The eggs, which are *c.* 2 mm in diameter, hatch in 5–8 days at a temperature of 22–26°C (72–79°F). The young can be fed at first on live food, such as micro-worms and *Artemia* nauplii, and growth is rapid. The eggs and young should be separated from the adults until the young have reached a length of *c.* 1 cm ($\frac{1}{3}$ in.). It is a fascinating sight to see a large 'family' of armoured catfishes of various sizes in a large, shallow aquarium tank.

The systematics of the group, particularly of the genus *Corydoras*, is under constant revision and it is possible that some of the 'species' are identical. Most of the forms mentioned here have the same requirements, so it is sufficient to give their size and distribution together with any points of special interest.

140. *Brochis coeruleus*
7 cm (2$\frac{3}{4}$ in.). Amazon near Iquitos. A very shy species.

141. *Corydoras aeneus*
Bronze Corydoras
7 cm (2$\frac{3}{4}$ in.). Trinidad and Venezuela, south to La Plata basin. Temperature 20–23°C (68–73°F).

142. *Corydoras arcuatus*
Arched Corydoras
5 cm (2 in.). Amazon near the town of Tefé.

143. *Corydoras axelrodi*
5 cm (2 in.). Rio Meta in Colombia.

144. *Corydoras barbatus*
Banded Corydoras
12 cm (4$\frac{3}{4}$ in.). From São Paulo to Rio de Janeiro.

145. *Corydoras caudimaculatus*
6 cm (2$\frac{1}{4}$ in.). Upper Rio Guapore.

146. *Corydoras elegans*
6 cm (2$\frac{1}{4}$ in.). Middle Amazon.

147. *Corydoras melini*
5 cm (2 in.). Rio Papuri.

148. *Corydoras metae*
5 cm (2 in.). Rio Meta, in the region of Baringana.

149. *Corydoras myersi*
Myers' Corydoras
6 cm (2$\frac{1}{4}$ in.). Amazon tributaries above the junction with the Rio Negro.

150. *Corydoras paleatus*
Peppered Corydoras
7 cm (2$\frac{3}{4}$ in.). South-eastern Brazil and La Plata. Temperature: 18–20°C (64–68°F).

151. *Corydoras schultzei*
6·5 cm (2$\frac{1}{2}$ in.). Tributaries of the Amazon. Probably closely related to No. 141.

152. *Corydoras cochui*
2·5 cm (1 in.). Central Brazil.

153. *Corydoras haraldschultzi*
7 cm (2$\frac{3}{4}$ in.). Rio Guapore.

154. *Corydoras hastatus*
   Dwarf Corydoras
3 cm (1¼ in.). Amazon, around Villa
Bella. A very free-swimming species.

155. *Corydoras julii*
   Leopard Corydoras
6 cm (2¼ in.). Lower Amazon
tributaries.

156. *Corydoras melanistius*
   Black-spotted Corydoras
6 cm (2¼ in.). Northern South
America.

157. *Corydoras punctatus*
6 cm (2¼ in.). Orinoco, Essequibo and
Amazon.

158. *Corydoras pygmaeus*
3 cm (1¼ in.). Brazil, but a more exact
locality is lacking. A lively species
often sold as *Corydoras hastatus*.

159. *Corydoras reticulatus*
   Reticulated Corydoras
7 cm (2¾ in.). Lower Amazon. A very
shy species.

160. *Corydoras schwartzi*
3 cm (1¼ in.). Distribution not
known.

161. *Corydoras undulatus*
5 cm (2 in.). Eastern Brazil and La
Plata.

162. *Dianema urostriata*
15 cm (6 in.). Large parts of the
Amazon region. A nocturnal species
which is said to build a bubble-nest.

163. *Hoplosternum thoracatum*
18–20 cm (7–7¾ in.). Panama to
Paraguay. With the large area of
distribution this species is very variable in appearance. Sex differences:
male smaller with a white belly
marked with round spots at spawning
time; the female is larger with the
foremost pectoral fin rays strongly
developed, and with a greyish-violet
belly at spawning time. This is a
crepuscular and nocturnal fish which
can be kept in a large tank with plenty
of hiding-places. Before pairing the
male builds a bubble-nest, in which
the female lays 800–1,000 eggs.
According to Knaack they hatch in
4 days, at a temperature of 23–24°C
(73–75°F). The female should be
removed after egg-laying. The male
tends the young for a time after
hatching.

Cyprinodontidae
Egg-laying Toothcarps, Killifishes
This family which contains about 500
species has a wide distribution in all
parts of the tropics and in many subtropical areas, but not in Australia.
In recent years a considerable amount
of work has been done to clarify the
systematics of the various species.
Almost all the species are small, and
are best kept in small tanks (5–20
litres, 1¾–5¼ U.S. gals) with several
females to each male. It is a good idea
to standardise the tanks and the
method of maintenance. The basic
points are: small, silicone-cemented
glass tanks arranged in series, and
fitted with tight-fitting glass lids.
Filtration and aeration are unneces-
sary. The substrate can be of coarse
sphagnum moss (previously boiled),
but never sand. The plants should be
fast-growing species such as *Synnema
triflorum* and *Ceratopteris*, and the
water ought to be hard (15–20° DH),
and neutral or slightly alkaline in
order to prevent attacks by fungi. The
main diet should be live and varied,
but most species will also take dried
food.
   There are two principal methods of

breeding in this family: 1) in the so-called seasonal or annual fishes the eggs require a period out of water before they will hatch, and 2) in the non-seasonal species the eggs develop in the water in the normal way.

For non-seasonal fishes the breeding tank should have clean water and a mop of nylon wool and nothing else. The breeding fish must have been kept separate for 1–2 weeks and given plenty of food; when they are introduced into the tank spawning will often take place within a few hours. The eggs are laid in the mop, and are allowed to harden for 3–4 hours after laying. The mop is then removed, the eggs shaken out or picked off and placed in shallow dishes containing the same type of water at the same temperature: 22–24°C (72–75°F). Methylene blue can be added to produce a distinct blue colour. The eggs hatch in 2–4 weeks. Unfertilised, mouldy or white eggs should be removed as a daily routine. The young should immediately be transferred to a rearing tank and fed on *Artemia* nauplii. In many species the rate of growth is not very uniform, so the young should be sorted according to size during the period of growth.

Seasonal species lay their eggs in the substrate. The breeding stock, usually several males and females, should be put into a tank with a thick layer of peat on the bottom. As soon as it appears that the substrate contains a sufficient number of eggs the breeding fishes should be removed and the content of the tank (water and substrate) should be poured through a strainer. As soon as the water has dripped out the substrate is spread out on to an absorbent underlay (newspaper) and allowed to dry at room temperature until it has a

crumbly consistency. The peat is then placed in a dated plastic bag, which is closed and kept in the dark at a temperature of 22–24°C (72–75°F). After a period of at least 4 weeks the contents of the bag are placed in a tank and water (clean rainwater is excellent) is poured over until the peat floats. The water temperature should be 18–22°C (64–72°F), and the floating layer not more than 5 cm (2 in.) thick. When they hatch the young can be reared like those of non-seasonal fishes. If the eggs do not hatch the whole procedure can be repeated.

In the following section the species are arranged in a number of subfamilies. If any special breeding conditions are necessary these are given under each species.

Cyprinodontinae

164. *Jordanella floridae*
American Flagfish

7 cm (2¾ in.). Florida and Yucatan. A hardy fish which will do best in a densely planted, sunlit tank with hard, alkaline water at a temperature of 20–24°C (68–75°F). The eggs are laid on the bottom where they are guarded by the male who fans fresh water over them until they hatch. Some 50–150 eggs may be laid at a time, and these hatch in 6–8 days. The young are quite easy to rear as they will take *Artemia* immediately. This species must be given a certain amount of vegetable food.

165. *Cyprinodon macularius*
Desert Pupfish

Male 7 cm (2¾ in.), female somewhat smaller. Basin of the lower Colorado and Gila Rivers and the Salton Sea, from southern Arizona to eastern lower California, and the Sonoyta River of northern Sonora, Mexico, in brackish and salt water. Temperature 18–23°C (64–73°F).

Aphaniinae

166. *Aphanius fasciatus*
6 cm (2¼ in.). Coastal areas of the Mediterranean from France to Turkey. A hardy, omnivorous species found in both fresh and salt water. It breeds as a non-seasonal fish, and the eggs hatch in 10–14 days.

Fundulinae
About 40 species distributed in the United States and Central America.

167. *Fundulus chrysotus*
   Golden Topminnow
8 cm (3 in.). South-eastern United States. Sex differences: the female has small silvery dots and is smaller than the male. Temperature: 20–23°C (68–73°F). Non-seasonal.

168. *Lucania goodei* (formerly
   Chriopeops goodei)
   Blue-fin Killifish
6 cm (2¼ in.). Florida. Sex difference: female paler than male. This species should be kept as a group in a densely planted aquarium tank with medium-hard water at a temperature of 18–23°C (64–73°F). The fish should be fed on live food, preferably gnat or mosquito larvae. This is a non-seasonal species, which can be bred in an ordinary aquarium tank, with plenty of surface vegetation. However, aquarium-bred specimens often lack the beautiful colours. This is one of the more difficult of the egg-laying toothcarps.

Rivulinae
This subfamily, with about 280 species, forms the largest group of killifishes. According to Scheel the

subfamily has three generic groups: 1) the Rivulidi with the genera *Rivulus, Trigonectes, Pterolebias* and *Rachovia*, 2) the Aplocheilidi with the genera *Aplocheilus* and *Pachypanchax*, 3) the Cynolebiatidi with the genera *Austrofundulus, Cynolebias* and *Cynopoecilus* in the New World and *Aphyosemion* and *Nothobranchius* in the Old World. The species show marked sexual dimorphism, the females being small and inconspicuous, olive or beige with small red dots and rounded fins, see No. 206, whereas the males are very brightly coloured with elongated or pointed fins. Some species are seasonal fishes, others non-seasonal.

169. *Pterolebias longipinnis*
10 cm (3¾ in.). Brazil. Possibly identical with *Pterolebias maculipinnis* which also comes from low-lying country east of the Andes. Breeds as a typical seasonal fish.

171. *Epiplatys annulatus/*
   Aplocheilus annulatus
9 cm (3½ in.). Western part of the Amazon region. Seasonal.

171. *Epiplatys annulatus/*
   Aplocheilus annulatus
   Rocket Panchax
4 cm (1½ in.). West Africa, Lower Guinea, Sierra Leone and western Liberia. A non-seasonal fish with variable coloration, which is not very easy to breed in the aquarium. The eggs are laid among the roots of floating plants, and the young are smaller than those of most other killifishes.

172. *Epiplatys bifasciatus/*
   Aplocheilus bifasciatus
5 cm (2 in.). West Africa, in streams in savanna country. A very stationary surface-living, non-seasonal fish.

173. *Epiplatys chaperi/*
    Aplocheilus chaperi
    Firemouth Epiplatys
6 cm (2¼ in.). Ghana and Ivory Coast.
See No. 172.

174. *Aplocheilus lineatus*
10 cm (3¾ in.). Southern India. A
rather peaceful, non-seasonal species,
with large eggs.

175. *Epiplatys sexfasciatus/*
    Aplocheilus sexfasciatus
    Six-barred Epiplatys
10 cm (3¾ in.). Ghana and Gabon. A
rather aggressive, non-seasonal fish,
showing considerable variation.

176. *Pachypanchax playfairi*
10 cm (3¾ in.). Seychelles and
Zanzibar. An aggressive, non-
seasonal species, with small eggs.

177. *Aphyosemion ahli*
    Ahl's Aphyosemion
6 cm (2¼ in.). Marshy areas along the
coast from western Nigeria to Lower
Zaïre. The coloration of the male
varies considerably from individual
to individual. The species of *Aphyosemion* should be kept and bred as
non-seasonal fishes, see p. 179.

178. *Aphyosemion arnoldi*
    Arnold's Lyretail
5 cm (2 in.). Niger delta. An attractive
but very delicate little fish.

179. *Aphyosemion australe*
    Cape Lopez Lyretail
5 cm (2 in.). Gabon and Congo
(Brazzaville), in marshy areas along
the coast. This is one of the earliest
known forms of *Aphyosemion*. In the
males the coloration, particularly the
red pattern on the flanks, is very
variable. It is probably a seasonal
fish in the wild, but the eggs will hatch
without a period out of water. The
selected form *Aphyosemion australe*

'*hjerreseni*' is golden-yellow with a
pattern of red dots.

180. *Aphyosemion bualanum*
5 cm (2 in.). Western central Africa,
in savanna streams. A hardy, non-
seasonal species. The young grow
very slowly.

181. *Roloffia bertholdi*
    [*Aphyosemion bertholdi*]
This fish may be regarded as belonging to the superspecies No. 197, and
most authors now place it in that
genus.

182. *Aphyosemion bivittatum*
    Red Lyretail
5 cm (2 in.). Lowlands from Togo to
Rio Muni, in savanna and forest
streams. The female is the only
Aphyosemion to have dark longitudinal stripes. A peaceful species
which is easy to keep, even in a
community tank. It is a non-seasonal
fish which breeds quite readily in the
aquarium.

183. '*Burundi aphyosemion*'
    ['*Aphyosemion burundi*']
5 cm (2 in.). Niger delta region, but
not in Burundi. This form has not yet
been given a valid scientific name.

184. *Aphyosemion calliurum*
    Red-chinned Aphyosemion
5 cm (2 in.). Coastal areas from
western Nigeria to the lower Zaïre.
Non-seasonal.

185. *Aphyosemion cameronense*
    [*Aphyosemion camerounense*]
6 cm (2¼ in.). East Cameroun to
Zaïre, in inland areas. Non-seasonal.

186. *Aphyosemion celiae*
    [*Aphyosemion celia*]
4 cm (1½ in.). West Cameroun. No
details are available on its requirements in the aquarium.

187. *Aphyosemion cinnamomeum*
5 cm (2 in.). From a limited mountain region in West Cameroun. A rather delicate, non-seasonal species.

188. *Aphyosemion cognatum*
5 cm (2 in.). Central parts of Zaïre. This hardy, non-seasonal form belongs to the superspecies *Aphyosemion elegans*.

189. *Aphyosemion exiguum*
5 cm (2 in.). Western central Africa, in forest streams. An attractive but somewhat difficult species which is non-seasonal. The young grow slowly.

190. *Aphyosemion christyi*
5 cm (2 in.). Central Zaïre. A non-seasonal fish, which like No. 188, belongs to the superspecies *Aphyosemion elegans*.

191. *Aphyosemion filamentosum*
Plumed Lyretail
5 cm (2 in.). Southern Nigeria and West Cameroun. Closely related to *Aphyosemion arnoldi* but not quite so delicate. Non-seasonal.

192. *Aphyosemion gardneri*
7 cm (2¾ in.). Nigeria and West Cameroun. This is a non-seasonal species which is said to be one of the easiest to breed. There are two kinds of male, one with yellow on the fins (No. 192 below) and one without (No. 192 above).

193. *Roloffia geryi*
   [*Aphyosemion geryi*]
5 cm (2 in.). Guinea and Sierra Leone. A slender, non-seasonal species which resembles No. 197.

194. *Roloffia guineensis*
   [*Aphyosemion guineense*]
7 cm (2¾ in.). Northern Sierra Leone, in mountain streams. A very coarse species, which rather resembles the species of *Pachypanchax*, and by some it is regarded as a link with this genus. Non-seasonal.

195. *Aphyosemion gulare*
   Yellow Gularis
8 cm (3 in.). Southern Nigeria. A very variable, non-seasonal species in which the male is characterised by the irregular fringed edge to the dorsal fin.

196. *Aphyosemion labarrei*
5 cm (2 in.). Zaïre. A non-seasonal form, often very aggressive.

197. *Roloffia liberiensis*
   [*Aphyosemion liberiense*]
5 cm (2 in.). West Africa. A superspecies which also contains No. 181 and No. 200. It should be kept and bred like the other non-seasonal species in the genus.

198. *Aphyosemion lujae*
5 cm (2 in.). A small area north of Kinshasa (formerly Léopoldville) in Zaïre. This species is often marketed under completely erroneous names. It is a peaceful form, but not very easy to breed. Non-seasonal.

199. *Roloffia occidentalis*
   [*Aphyosemion occidentale*]
9 cm (3½ in.). Sierra Leone. Often wrongly known as *Aphyosemion sjoestedti* (No. 202). A large, voracious and extremely brightly coloured species. This is a seasonal fish, so the eggs should be allowed to rest for a couple of months as described on page 179.

200. *Roloffia roloffi*
   [*Aphyosemion roloffi*]
5 cm (2 in.). A form within the superspecies No. 197.

201. *Aphyosemion santaisabellae*
    [*Aphyosemion santa-isabellae*]
5 cm (2 in.). Streams east of Santa
Isabella, the capital of Fernando Po.
This fish can be bred as a non-seasonal
species, but the percentage of eggs
hatched is said to rise if it is treated as a
seasonal form.

202. *Aphyosemion sjoestedti*
    Blue Gularis
12 cm (4¾ in.). Southern Nigeria and
West Cameroun, in swampy areas.
This, the largest African killifish,
should be kept and bred as No.
199.

203. *Aphyosemion walkeri*
7 cm (2¾ in.). Southern Ghana and
Ivory Coast. Closely related to
Aphyosemion gardneri but more delicate and more difficult to breed.

204. *Austrofundulus dolichopterus*
5 cm (2 in.). Venezuela, in small shady
pools. This is a seasonal fish which
rarely reaches an age of more than one
year. The coloration of the males
varies from a delicate violet to rust-
brown. The females are considerably
paler with the unpaired fins less
pointed and produced. Spawning
takes place just above the bottom
(sphagnum) and the eggs develop as
described under seasonal fishes, page
179. The resting period of the eggs
is about 5 months. The young can
immediately take *Artemia*.

205. *Cynolebias belottii*
    [*Cynolebias belotti*]
7 cm (2¾ in.). Rio de la Plata region
in Argentina, Paraguay and Uruguay.
The optimum temperature range is
16–22°C (61–72°F). Spawning takes
place on the bottom, and extends over
a period of 8–10 days. The eggs of
this seasonal fish should rest for about
3 months. The young grow very

rapidly and are sexually mature at 2
months.

206. *Cynolebias nigripinnis*
    Argentine Pearl Fish
5 cm (2 in.). Various localities in
Argentina. More elegant and more
brightly coloured than No. 205.
Otherwise as for No. 206 but the
water temperature should not fall
below 18°C (64°F).

207. *Cynolebias whitei*
8 cm (3 in.). Brazil, in the area of Rio
de Janeiro. During pairing, which
takes place in the substrate, the female
places her head in under one of the
male's pectoral fins. Otherwise as for
No. 205.

208. *Nothobranchius guentheri*
    [*Nothobranchius orthonotus*]
7 cm (2¾ in.). Temporary pools in
Zanzibar. The species of *Nothobranchius* are seasonal fishes which
occur in nature in small sunlit,
turbid pools, in which the water
temperature may fluctuate considerably during the course of 24 hours.
They are very brightly coloured and
aggressive fishes which should be kept
without other species, but even then
are not easy to keep. They should be
treated as seasonal fishes, and the
eggs should be allowed to rest for
about 2 months. According to
Pinter, however, the eggs of *Nothobranchius* can also be treated like those
of non-seasonal fishes.

209. *Nothobranchius palmquisti*
5 cm (2 in.). Coastal lowlands of
Tanzania. Care and breeding as for
No. 208.

210. *Nothobranchius rachovii*
    [*Nothobranchius rachovi*]
5 cm (2 in.). Mozambique. Care and
breeding as for No. 208.

211. *Fundulosoma thierryi*
[*Nothobranchius thierryi*]
3–4 cm (1¼–1½ in.). West Africa, in pools in the savanna. Care and breeding as for No. 208.

Procatopodinae
An interesting subfamily, with species ranging over large areas of Africa, so their habits are varied and they require different types of care in the aquarium. They are all shoaling fishes which live near to the water surface. The savannah species are easier to deal with than those from forest streams, which often panic when there are sudden changes in aquarium lighting. In addition the forest species are more frequently attacked by fungus and *Oodinium* (a parasitic protozoan).

These fishes thrive best in hard, alkaline water with frequent changes of up to a quarter of the volume. Breeding is most successful in slightly alkaline, bacteria-free water with a hardness of about 10–14° DH. Some authors recommend the addition of 10–15 per cent sea water. At spawning time 2–20 eggs are laid per day over a period of about 2 weeks. The eggs of the *Aplocheilichthys* species are laid in holes or among roots. At 25°C (77°F) they hatch in about 2 weeks and the fry rise to just below the surface, where they can be fed on very live food and finely powdered dried food. The young are seldom attacked by the parents. These species can be bred either as seasonal fishes or as described for non-seasonal fishes on page 179, after the eggs have hardened for 3–4 hours. With good feeding they should be fully grown in 5–6 months.

212. *Procatopus nototaenia*
[*Procatopus similis*]
5 cm (2 in.). Nigeria and Cameroun, near the coast. According to Scheel

the genus *Procatopus* has two good zoological species.

213. *Aplocheilichthys macrophthalmus*
4 cm (1½ in.). Rain-forest streams from southern Togo to southern Cameroun and at Lagos in south-western Nigeria.

214. *Aplocheilichthys schioetzi*
5 cm (2 in.). West Africa, savanna areas. In addition to these two species there are several others, but the systematics of the genus is still not fully understood. Only No. 213 has become widely distributed as an aquarium fish.

Oryziatinae
A small Asiatic subfamily containing one genus with ten known species, which are so similar to one another that they are often difficult to identify. The genus is distributed in tidal waters from southern China and Japan through Sri Lanka (Ceylon), Malaya, the Philippines and the larger Indonesian islands to India. Care and breeding as for the Procatopodinae. The very large eggs hang in clusters from the female's cloaca until they are scraped off against plants. The number of eggs varies from about 200 in *Oryzias latipes* to 3–4 in *O. minutillus* which is scarcely 2 cm (¾ in.) long.

215. *Oryzias javanicus*
4 cm (1½ in.). Malaya and some of the Indonesian islands.

Poeciliidae
Live-bearing Toothcarps
The live-bearing toothcarps range from southern North America through Central America to the tropical and subtropical regions of South America. In nature most species live in small sunlit lakes and ponds

with dense vegetation. Some species occur in brackish waters in the vicinity of estuaries. The family contains many of the best known and most popular aquarium fishes. On account of the variation in hereditary characters, many species have been subjected to hybridisation and selection, and nowadays there are enormous numbers of domesticated forms, but these do not always breed true. Most of the live-bearing toothcarps are hardy and attractive fishes, which are suitable both for the beginner and for the more experienced breeder.

This family, together with a few others, has a special condition, in that live young are produced which have gone through their embryonic development within the body of the female. The male's anal fin is modified to form a copulatory organ or gonopodium. This organ can be turned forwards during mating, and through it sperms or a capsule of sperms, known as a spermatophore, are transferred from the male into the genital opening of the female. The sperms can remain viable in the female's oviduct for over a year. At intervals of 3–5 weeks new eggs develop and these are usually fertilised within the ovary of the female. There is no exchange of nutritive materials between the female and the developing eggs which obtain their nourishment from their own yolk. The whole process may be regarded as a form of ordinary incubation, except that it takes place within the female. When development is complete, the young are released to the outside world, either just hatched or ready to hatch. Immediately after their release from the female the young move up to the surface to fill their swimbladder with air. The Least Killifish, *Heterandria formosa*, is an exception, for here the female has numerous embryos of different ages and these are released in batches of 2–3 every few days.

The live-bearing toothcarps are not difficult to keep, provided they are given clean, slightly alkaline and hard water, plenty of plant food and the appropriate temperature (see under the individual species).

In most species the parents do not attack the young, which can be reared in the same tank. This does not apply to *Gambusia, Xiphophorus helleri helleri* and especially not to *Belonesox*. For these species a spawning box should be used. A long tank is positioned so that one end is away from the light. The spawning box with the breeding female is placed at this darker end of the tank. After birth the young swim towards the light and thus away from the female.

The young are not difficult to rear provided they are given a plentiful supply of food right from the start. It is best to start with *Artemia*, micro-worms and powdered dry vegetable food. They should, if possible, be fed several times a day. Every 14 days about one-third of the water in the rearing tank should be removed and replaced with fresh water. Although the live-bearing toothcarps are, in general, easy to keep and breed, this does not mean that the aquarist can afford to be negligent during the period of rearing and feeding the young. In recent years many aquarium strains of these attractive fishes have undergone a reduction in size, not least because of insufficient feeding during the period of growth.

Species or genetically true domesticated forms should not be hybridised, unless one has a special reason. Nowadays, in fact, it seems that there is greater need for improvement of the existing species and forms than for new domesticated types.

216. *Belonesox belizanus*
Pike Topminnow
Male 10 cm (3¾ in.), female 20 cm (7¾ in.). Central America, occurring in some places in brackish water. An extremely predatory, surface-living species, which feeds mainly on other fishes and large insect larvae. It should be kept in a large aquarium tank, with patches of dense vegetation but without other fishes. Temperature 25–30°C (77–86°F). The female produces up to 100 young at a time, and these are *c.* 2·5 cm (1 in.) long. They are subject to continual attack by the adults.

217. *Gambusia affinis affinis*
Male 3·5 cm (1¼ in.), female 6 cm (2¼ in.). Southern United States and northern Mexico. A very hardy species which tolerates temperatures from 6–30°C (43–86°F). It can be kept at room temperature. These are, however, aggressive fishes and should be kept in a tank on their own.

218. *Gambusia affinis holbrooki*
Male 3 cm (1¼ in.), female 6 cm (2¼ in.). From New Jersey to Florida and California. Otherwise as for the preceding species.

219. *Girardinus metallicus*
Girardinus
Male 5 cm (2 in.), female 8 cm (3 in.). Cuba. Temperature: 22–25°C (72–77°F). Up to 60 young born at a time.

220. *Heterandria formosa*
Least Killifish
Male 2 cm (¾ in.), female 3·5 cm (1¼ in.). South Carolina, Georgia and Florida. Temperature: 19–24°C (66–75°F). This tiny species should be kept in a tank on its own. The female produces 2–3 young every third day or so over a period of about 3 weeks.

The young are not attacked by the adults.

221. *Phalloceros caudimaculatus reticulatus*
Caudo
Male 2·5 cm (1 in.), female 6 cm (2¾ in.). Brazil, Uruguay and Paraguay. Temperature: 20–24°C (68–75°F). Up to 80 young produced at a time.

222. *Poecilia melanogaster/ Limia melanogaster*
Blue Limia
Male 3 cm (1¼ in.), female 6 cm (2¼ in.). Jamaica. The female has a conspicuous 'pregnancy mark', hence the specific name *melanogaster* (black belly). Temperature: 25–28°C (77–82°F). Up to 80 young born at a time.

223. *Poecilia nigrofasciata/ Limia nigrofasciata*
Black-barred Limia
Male 5 cm (2 in.), female 6 cm (2¼ in.). Haiti. The male develops a hump back with age, and his tail becomes larger. A very attractive but somewhat rare species. Temperature: 23–28°C (73–82°F). Up to 50 born at a time. Rather susceptible to bacterial infections.

224. *Poecilia reticulata/ Lebistes reticulatus*
Guppy
Male 3 cm (1¼ in.), female 6 cm (2¼ in.). Venezuela, Barbados, Trinidad, northern Brazil and Guyana. In certain places it occurs in brackish water, and under experimental conditions it can even be acclimatised to salt water, with a specific gravity up to 1·025.

The hardiness and readiness to breed of the guppy, together with the very variable colours and patterns of the male, have made this species one of the most popular of all aquarium fishes. These characteristics have also made it suitable as an experimental animal for genetical research. It is now possible to correlate certain markings with definite genes on the chromosomes. The production of pure guppy strains entails years of systematic selection from batch after batch of young. As a result of this intensive inbreeding many of the so-called improved strains have become delicate and susceptible to disease. To a certain extent this degeneration can be avoided if the breeder works with several lines of the same strain, which are kept apart, so that at certain intervals a male from one line can be mated with a female from another.

It would not be possible within the scope of this book to describe the practical details of so-called guppy improvement, but the reader is referred to the specialist literature (see p. 237). The following basic points are, however, relevant: 1) Long-term breeding to improve the ornamental guppy requires a male and a female of the same strain. 2) The food should be plentiful and varied, and one-third of the water should be replaced with fresh water at frequent intervals. The water should have a pH of *c*.7, a hardness of 15–24° DH, and be kept at a temperature of 25–27°C (77–81°F). 3) The strains should be kept separate. 4) After birth the young should be separated from the parents and reared in spacious tanks. 5) The young should be separated according to sex as soon as the gonopodium of the males develops. 6) All genetically unsuitable fish should be eliminated. 7) Matings should only be allowed between brother and sister, father and daughter or mother and son. Illustration No. 224 shows: A) The wild form with female to the right. B) Round Tail Golden Guppy and below a female Golden Guppy with a special tail pattern. C) 'Snakeskin' Guppy. (*a*) Round Tail. (*b*) Robson Round Tail. (*c*) Round Tail Golden Guppy. (*d*) Speartail. (*e*) Pintail. (*f*) Lyretail. (*g*) Double Sword Golden Guppy. (*h*) Bottom Sword. (*i*) Top Sword. (*j*) Flagtail. (*k*) Veiltail. (*l*) Triangle. (*m*) Fantail.

225. *Poecilia sphenops/*
Mollienesia sphenops
Pointed-mouth Molly/
Sphenops Molly

Male 8 cm (3 in.), female 12 cm (4¾ in.). From Mexico to Colombia in fresh and brackish waters. The males vary considerably in appearance. No. 225 shows a young, uncoloured male, 225a a coloured male and 225b the popular black domesticated form, known as the Liberty Molly. It is possible that the new Lyretail Molly has also been developed from *Poecilia sphenops*.

This species requires a spacious tank, a plentiful vegetarian diet, and clean, clear water at a temperature of 26–29°C (79–84°F). The female produces up to 80 young at a time.

226. *Poecilia velifera*
Sailfin Molly

15 cm (6 in.). Yucatan, in the vicinity of the coasts and in river estuaries. Care as for No. 225, but this species should not be kept in tanks with a capacity of less than 15 litres (4 U.S. gals) if the males are to develop their handsome dorsal fins. The Black Velifera or Midnight Molly is a handsome variety of *Poecilia velifera* which is jet-black with a yellow or orange edge to the dorsal fin. There are numerous domesticated forms of this species.

227. *Poecilia vittata*
Cuban Limia
Male 6·5 cm (2½ in.), female 10 cm (3¾ in.). Cuba. For care see family description. Temperature: 22–25°C (72–77°F). Up to 200 young produced at a time.

228. *Priapella intermedia*
Male 5 cm (2 in.), female 6–7 cm (2¼–2¾ in.). Mexico, Tehuantepec. An attractive, but delicate, small shoaling fish, which should be kept by itself in a spacious tank. Temperature: 24–26°C (75–79°F). Otherwise as given under the family description. Up to 20 young born at a time. Males are often produced in greater numbers than females.

229. *Xiphophorus helleri helleri*
Swordtail
Male 8 cm (3 in.) excluding sword, female 12 cm (4¾ in.). South-eastern Mexico and Guatemala. One of the classical live-bearers, characterised by its hardiness and by the sword-like elongation of the caudal fin rays in the male. This is a very variable species which can be hybridised with No. 230. This has given rise to numerous varieties and selected forms of the original green Swordtail. In the illustration the bottom blue-black fish and the red fish (top right) may be hybrids between *Xiphophorus helleri helleri* and *X. maculatus*.

Unlike the other live-bearing toothcarps, *X. helleri helleri* has no sex chromosomes. The genes determining sex are distributed on the other chromosomes (autosomes). Young, sexually immature Swordtails carry the potentialities of both sexes. They develop either into sexually mature females or into small, very slender males. Development to maleness may also proceed via an anatomically typical female, which changes its sex to become a large type of male. Females mated with these larger males produce a much greater percentage of females than those mated with the smaller males.

Swordtails should be kept as described under the family. Temperature: 22–26°C (72–79°F). Up to 180 young may be produced at a time.

230. *Xiphophorus maculatus*
Platy
Male 4 cm (1½ in.), female 6 cm (2¼ in.). Mexico and Guatemala. The illustration shows four hybrid forms: above to the left, a female of the Black Platy; above to the right, a male of the Golden Wagtail Platy (also found as a red form with black fins, the Red Wagtail Platy); below to the left, a Red Platy; and below to the right, the Tuxedo Platy. In addition, there are long-finned platies and numerous other colour varieties. Up to 80 young produced at a time.

231. *Xiphorus variatus*
Variatus Platy
Male 5·5 cm (2⅛ in.), females 7 cm (2¾ in.). Mexico, to the north of the range of No. 230. A very attractive and in the wild very variable species, which has been subject to a great amount of 'improvement' in the aquarium. Up to 100 young produced at a time.

Anablepidae
Foureyes
This family has one genus with three species in the fresh and brackish waters of southern Mexico, Central America and northern South America.

232. *Anableps anableps*
Foureyes
17 cm (6¾ in.). A typical surface-living fish, in which the eyes are so constructed that when lying at the

surface it can see above and below the water. This unique adaptation is due to the horizontal division of the pupil and retina.

Another peculiar character of this live-bearing fish is that in 50 per cent of the females the genital opening opens to the right and in 50 per cent to the left. Accordingly, the gonopodia of the males turn either to the left or to the right during mating. In other words, 'left-turning' males can only mate with 'right-turning' females and vice versa.

This species should be kept in large shallow tanks, with a capacity over 250 litres (65½ U.S. gals) and with a large free surface area and patches of dense vegetation. Temperature: 23–25°C (73–77°F). The fish should be fed on a variety of living insects which are taken from the surface and on small fish, water fleas and dried food which will also be consumed at the surface. At birth the young are 3–5 cm (1¼–2 in.) long, and the female produces up to six at a time. Foureyes may be aggressive towards other members of their own species, but are completely peaceful with other species of their own size.

Hemiramphidae
Halfbeaks

A tropical and subtropical family with several species found mainly in the sea and in brackish waters, and with only a couple of species in fresh water. Some of the species are live-bearers.

233. *Dermogenys pusillus*
Halfbeak

Male 6 cm. (2½ in.), female 7 cm (2¾ in.). Thailand, Malaya, Singapore and the larger Indonesian islands, in both fresh and brackish water, most commonly in slow-flowing streams. Sex difference (apart from the size):

the red colour of the male's dorsal fin is lacking in the female. Typical surface-living fishes which should be kept in a large, shallow tank with plenty of floating vegetation. Halfbeaks do best in hard, alkaline water, with or without the addition of 2 teaspoonfuls of sea salt per 10 litres (2½ U.S. gals) of water. Temperature: 22–26°C (72–79°F). They should be fed mainly on insects (fruit-flies and gnat larvae) but will also take water fleas (*Daphnia*). They are very aggressive towards one another, and they sometimes panic and damage the long lower jaw by swimming against the aquarium glass.

Halfbeaks will only breed successfully if given plenty of live food. The very large young (7–11 mm, *c.* ⅓ in.) should be reared in tanks with shallow water and a good supply of *Cyclops* and *Diaptomus* nauplii or of *Artemia*. Well-fed females will produce young, up to 25 at a time, at intervals of about 30 days.

Syngnathidae
Pipefishes
See also p. 234.

234. *Syngnathus pulchellus*

15 cm (6 in.). Zaïre, Ogowe, in both fresh and brackish waters. These fish should be kept in a spacious tank with good lighting and they do best in hard, alkaline water containing two teaspoonfuls of sea salt per 10 litres (2½ U.S. gals) of fresh water. They prefer to live in among the narrow leaves of plants such as *Vallisneria*. Temperature: 23–25°C (73–77°F). They take all kinds of small, live food, but are difficult to breed.

Centrarchidae
Sunfishes
Perch-like, cold-water fishes from North America, which were at one time popular in the aquarium. The

189

following two species are still kept by some home aquarists.

235. *Elassoma evergladei*
Everglades Pigmy Sunfish
[Pigmy Sunfish]

3·5 cm (1½ in.). North Carolina to Florida. An interesting little fish which should be kept by itself in a small, well-planted but unheated aquarium tank. They should be fed principally on live food. Breeding, which takes place in the spring and summer months, starts with the male cavorting up and down in front of the female. At this time the male is velvet-black with an area of shining green scales on each side of the body. Mating takes place in among fine-leaved plants, and the female lays 6–8 eggs at a time, with a total of up to 50–60. The eggs hatch in about 3 days. The young, which are free-swimming on the seventh day, stay in among vegetation near the bottom and can be fed immediately on *Artemia*. They are not attacked by the parent fish and can be reared in the breeding tank. It is often recommended that this species should be kept at a temperature of 10–15°C (50–59°F) during the winter as this leads to improved breeding results.

236. *Enneacanthus chaetodon*
[*Mesogonistius chaetodon*]
Blackbanded Sunfish

10 cm (3¾ in.). New Jersey to Maryland. Sex difference: only apparent during the breeding season when the females are more brightly coloured. These fish should be kept in unheated tanks with dense patches of fine-leaved plants. This is a very stationary fish which should be fed on live food. In April–July the male makes one or more shallow pits in the bottom sand and this is followed by spawning. When the female has laid 200–500 eggs the male chases her away and takes over the care of the brood, fanning fresh water over the eggs. The female should be removed from the tank, although some aquarists say that this is not necessary. Depending upon the temperature the eggs hatch in 3–8 days. The young are swept out of the pit and they then hang for a few days among the plants. It is possible to remove the parent fish immediately after they have spawned, and to feed the fry on *Artemia* as soon as they have hatched. Rearing is not difficult, provided the young are given live food.

Centropomidae
Most of the species in this family occur in the sea or in brackish waters from East Africa to the island groups of the Indo-Pacific. Even the freshwater species appreciate the addition of a little salt to their tank water. There is still some confusion on the systematics and naming of the fishes in this family.

237. *Chanda ranga*
Indian Glassfish

5–6 cm (2–2¼ in.). Fresh and brackish waters in India, Burma and Thailand. Sex differences: the females are considerably paler than the males and they lack the pale blue edges to the dorsal and anal fins. These are attractive, hardy fish which thrive best in a spacious tank (80–100 litres, 21–26½ U.S. gals) with hard, alkaline water, containing two teaspoonfuls of salt per 10 litres (2½ U.S. gals) of water. Temperature: 19–24°C (66–75°F). They should be fed on live food.

The tank should be densely planted and well lit, as sunlight stimulates breeding activity. Spawning takes place at a temperature of 23–25°C

(73–77°F) in among fine-leaved plants or among the roots of floating plants, usually in the early morning. A large female may lay up to 500 eggs, and these are seldom eaten by the adults. This species is often bred in a small tank (20–40 litres, 5¼–10½ U.S. gals), and the parent fish are removed after spawning. The eggs, which are slightly sticky, hatch in about 24 hours and the young are free-swimming 1–2 days later. These are very small and they should be fed immediately on the nauplii of *Cyclops*, or better still of *Diaptomus*. The fry are very stationary and it may be difficult to maintain a sufficient concentration of food around them, so as to prevent them dying of hunger. This is best achieved by having shallow water and gentle aeration which moves the food around. After about 2 weeks the young can be fed on *Artemia* and from then on are not difficult to rear.

238. *Gynochanda filamentosa*
5 cm (2 in.). Malaya. Care and breeding as for the preceding species. According to Pinter, although this fish has been bred in the aquarium, the male's fins do not grow to their full length in captive-bred specimens.

Toxotidae
Archerfishes
A small family with species living in tidal areas from the Red Sea in the west to Australia and the Indonesian islands in the east. They are known as archerfishes because of their ability to shoot down insects perched on plants above the water. This is done by expelling drops of water from the mouth. The roof of the mouth has a groove which lies above a similar groove in the tongue, and the two together form a tube. By closing the gill-covers water is pressed through

this narrow barrel and leaves the mouth as a fast-moving drop that stuns the prey which falls into the water; the drops may travel for up to 1½ metres (*c.* 4½ ft). The shooting is generally very accurate, and it is significant that, as its eyes are just below water, the fish has to compensate for the difference in refraction between air and water.

In the young there is an iridescent yellow marking on each side of the back, and this probably serves as a signal which helps to keep others of the species in contact in the turbid waters of estuaries and mangrove swamps. The adults, which live solitarily, do not have these markings.

239. *Toxotes jaculatrix/*
    Toxotesjaculator
    Archerfish
24 cm (9½ in.). Found over large areas of the eastern part of the family's range. In captivity, Archerfish should be kept in large tanks half filled with water, which may be fresh, brackish or pure sea water. Temperature: 26–28°C (79–82°F). They will shoot down houseflies or fragments of fish or meat which are left on the tank glass above the water surface. They will also eat small fish and fry. They are often very shy and may be aggressive towards other members of their own species. They have never been bred in captivity.

Monodactylidae
Fingerfishes
A small family of tall, laterally compressed fishes, which occur in coastal waters of Africa, southern Asia and Australia.

240. *Monodactylus argenteus*
    Mono or Fingerfish
23 cm (9 in.). From East Africa to Malaya. When very small this species

can be kept in fresh water, but specimens over 6 cm (2¼ in.) long should be kept in pure sea water in a very large tank. Otherwise these are hardy, omnivorous fish which lose their attractive lemon-yellow colours and tall form as they grow older. Never bred in captivity.

241. *Monodactylus sebae*
Striped Fingerfish
20 cm (7¾ in.). West Africa, from Senegal to Zaïre. In general, very similar to the preceding species. Specimens up to 5 cm (2 in.) long should be kept in hard water with 3 teaspoonfuls of sea salt added per 10 litres (2½ U.S. gals); larger fish do not need salt provided the water is hard and slightly alkaline (pH *c.* 7·5). Wesley Wey of Mission Hills, California, has repeatedly spawned several pairs. The fish are mature when *c.* 10 cm (4 in.) long. Breeders must be well conditioned with live foods. Spawning begins with the pair chasing each other; finally they rapidly circle each other, the female releasing her ova, the male fertilising them. The parents are avid egg-eaters. The transparent pelagic eggs, *c.* ⅔ mm (*c.* $\frac{1}{36}$ in.) in diameter, hatch in 18–24 hours and must be in water with a specific gravity of at least 1·004 to develop properly. The larvae take *Artemia* nauplii and grow rapidly. Spawns of 25,000–60,000 are reported.

Scatophagidae
Argus Fishes
A small family of brackish-water fishes, which occur in the vicinity of estuaries in south-east Asia and northern Australia; from time to time they are found in fresh and sea water. They are mostly imported as young which are only 2·5–4 cm (1–1½ in.) long, and these can be kept in fresh water for some months. They grow rapidly. In nature they often feed exclusively on human faeces cast into the rivers. In the aquarium they should be given animal food with a supplement of vegetable matter, in the form of spinach or lettuce.

According to a single observation, the young of these fishes are protected by both parents, but there is no full account of their breeding.

242. *Scatophagus argus*
Scat or Argus Fish
30 cm (11½ in.). Distribution and care as given in the family description.

Badidae U.S.A.
Nandidae Britain
243. *Badis badis*
Badis
8 cm (3 in.). Large areas of India, in standing waters. Very variable in coloration. Sex differences: female usually paler than male. Females ready to spawn are also somewhat stouter. *Badis badis* is extremely peaceful, and often very shy although at spawning time the males indulge in territorial fighting. Temperature: 25–27°C (77–81°F). The eggs are laid in cavities and rock crevices, and are guarded by the male; in the aquarium flowerpots can be offered as spawning sites. The eggs hatch in 3 days and the young hang for a further 2 days from the roof of the cave. The adults should be removed as soon as the young are free-swimming. The young should at first be fed on *Artemia*.

244. *Badis badis burmanicus*
A colour variety of No. 243, described by Ahl in 1936.

Nandidae
A small family of small fishes with representatives in South America, Asia and Africa, but probably with a wider distribution in earlier periods of

the earth's history. The majority have a tall body, well developed spiny rays in the dorsal and anal fins and a very large mouth. They are well camouflaged, predatory and mostly rather stationary fishes which live in standing or slow-flowing waters and feed principally on other fishes. In the aquarium they should be able to shelter in among rocks and branches and the substrate should not be too pale.

245. *Monocirrhus polyacanthus*
South American Leaf-fish

8 cm (3 in.). Amazon and Rio Negro, western Guyana. No external sex differences. A very stationary, extremely predatory fish. In nature when it allows itself to be swept along by the current this fish looks like a withered leaf. When a prey animal is close enough it shoots out its mouth, which is enormous in relation to its size. It may seize fishes up to two-thirds of its own length.

This species should be kept in a large tank planted with Amazon Sword plants (*Echinodorus*), in soft water (hardness 2–6° DH) at pH 6–6·5 and a temperature of 22–25°C (72–77°F); the water should be kept moving by circulation or aeration. The eggs are laid on previously cleaned stones or leaves, and are guarded by the male. They hatch in about 3 days and the young remain hanging for a further 3–4 days. The young are large and they can immediately take *Artemia*. They should be sorted out according to size as they grow otherwise they will eat each other.

246. *Nandus nandus*
Nandus

20 cm (7¾ in.). India, Burma and Thailand. Care as given in the family description.

247. *Polycentropsis abbreviata*
African Leaf-fish

8 cm (3 in.). West Africa, Lagos, Niger and Ogowe. Care as given for the family. The sexes can only be distinguished externally at spawning time when the female is paler than the male. They do well in all types of water, and breed in soft, slightly acid water, see No. 245. The male builds a loose nest of bubbles, often among floating leaves. During spawning the female turns on her back beneath the nest and lays a single egg at a time.

The eggs (up to 100) adhere to floating plants by a small stalk. According to Pinter the eggs may also be laid on large leaves or rocks in the aquarium tank. The male protects the brood, and the female should be removed from the tank as soon as she has finished spawning. The eggs hatch in 48 hours, and the young are transferred by the male to a shallow pit in the sand where he guards them for a couple of days after they are free-swimming. The young are very voracious.

248. *Polycentrus schomburgki*
Schomburgk's Leaf-fish

8–10 cm (3–3¾ in.). North-eastern South America and Trinidad. Sexes only distinguishable during the breeding period, see illustration. Water type not critical. Temperature 23–28°C (73–82°F). The eggs are laid in holes or in flowerpots. The male undertakes most of the brood protection duties. The young are not difficult to rear but they are very voracious, and the smaller ones are frequently eaten by the larger.

Cichlidae
Cichlids

A family with about 1,000 known species, distributed in Central and tropical South America, and in

Africa where most of the species occur. There are two species of the genus *Etroplus* in Asia. Anatomically the cichlids are distinguished from related families in part by having only a single nostril on each side of the head. The cichlids have become adapted to a wide range of living conditions and in nature they occur in soft or hard, stationary or flowing waters. Some species even occur in brackish water. In view of their widely different habits and bright colours certain cichlids have become very popular among aquarists.

When adult most of the species are aggressive, territorial fishes which live in pairs or in small groups. Before they are sexually mature the majority live in shoals. The pairs eventually separate out from these, and this is a point which should be borne in mind when buying cichlids.

The cichlids practise brood protection, and according to its type they can be divided into two main groups: 1) Those that lay eggs out in the open on rocks or leaves. In this group the males and females are similar, i.e. there is no pronounced sexual dimorphism. The eggs are small and numerous and both parents take part in the care of eggs and young. 2) Species which keep their eggs hidden in one way or another. This group can be divided into two sub-groups: (*a*) Those which lay their eggs in holes or rock crevices. The male and female are usually different in size (the male being smaller) and coloration, i.e. there is sexual dimorphism. The female protects the brood; the eggs and the newly hatched young are relatively large and the total broods very small in comparison with those which spawn out in the open. (*b*) Mouth-brooding species, in which the female lays eggs in shallow pits dug by the male. The female then takes the eggs into her mouth and carries them in this way until they hatch.

This analysis, established by Wickler, applies with certain exceptions to all the species in the family. Details on care and other points are given under the individual genera and species.

Aequidens

A small South American genus of typical open-spawning species which can be kept in a planted aquarium tank, because they do not dig up the substrate. Water type not critical. Temperature: 25–27°C (77–81°F). Diet: live food and small pieces of chopped meat.

249. *Aequidens curviceps*
      Flag Cichlid
7–8 cm (2¾–3 in.). Amazon region. The smallest of the species in this genus. Sex difference: dorsal and anal fin drawn out to more of a point in the male than in the female. A very attractive and peaceful dwarf cichlid which prefers live food. This species is is often attacked by *Ichthyophonus* disease.

250. *Aequidens itanyi*
14 cm (5½ in.). Tributaries of the River Itany near the Surinam–French Guiana border. The dorsal and anal fins are drawn out to more of a point in the male than in the female. For care see the description of the genus. Up to 400 eggs laid at a time.

251. *Aequidens pulcher*
      [*Aequidens latifrons*]
      Blue Acara
17 cm (6¾ in.), but seldom more than 13 cm (5 in.) in the aquarium. Trinidad, Panama, northern Vene-

zuela, Colombia. An attractive cichlid which should be kept in a large tank as described under the genus. Up to 500 eggs laid at a time.

252. Aequidens maronii
Keyhole Cichlid

10 cm (3¾ in.). Guyana. Sex difference: not striking outside the spawning period; the male's dorsal and anal fins perhaps a little longer and more pointed than those of the female. A very peaceful species. It is very important to obtain several juveniles in order that they can sort themselves out into good, matching pairs. The young are not so easy to rear as those of the other species of Aequidens.

Apistogramma

A South American genus of typical 'egg-hiding' species with marked sexual dimorphism. In aquarium terms these fishes belong among the dwarf cichlids, which do not exceed 10–12 cm (3¾–4¾ in.) in length. The tanks need not be particularly large and a capacity of 50–80 litres (13¼–21 U.S. gals) is sufficient for a pair or for one male and two or three females. The substrate should be coarse sand. The species of Apistogramma need patches of dense vegetation and hiding-places provided by tree roots, rock crevices, flowerpots or coconut shells. Most species thrive in ordinary tap water filtered through sphagnum moss so that it is slightly acid. The water should, if possible, be kept moving by circulation or aeration. Temperature: 24–26°C (75–79°F). Live food is absolutely essential if these fishes are to thrive. With good care and feeding they are not difficult to breed. The female spawns in a hole or crevice and undertakes normal brood protection alone, although now and again the male may play a

part in this. Normally, however, the male should be removed at the end of spawning.

The newly hatched young can be fed at first on *Artemia* nauplii and after 14 days on small *Cyclops*. Growth is rapid and is improved if about a quarter of the water is replaced every 14 days.

In large aquarium tanks one can observe the territorial behaviour of these fishes. The males are polygamous and they set up territories which include the smaller territories of several females. In this way a harem colony is established in which the females defend their own territories within a single male's territory.

253 Apistogramma agassizi
Agassiz's Dwarf Cichlid

Male 7–8 cm (2¾–3 in.), female 5 cm (2 in.). Amazon region. Care as given in the description of the genus. There is a tendency for males to be in in the majority in a brood.

254. Apistogramma cacatuoides
[Apistogramma borelli]
Cockatoo Dwarf Cichlid
[Borelli's Dwarf Cichlid]

Male 8 cm (3 in.), female 4 cm (1½ in.). Mato Grosso region, Rio Paraguay and northern Argentina. This species should be kept as recommended in the description of the genus, but it likes a temperature of about 27°C (81°F).

255. Apistogramma ortmanni
Ortmann's Dwarf Cichlid

Male 7–8 cm (2¾–3 in.), female 4 cm (1½ in.). Western Guyana and the central part of the Amazon region. Sex differences: female smaller and paler than male, and with smaller fins. Care and breeding as given under the genus. Temperature: 26–28°C (79–82°F).

256. *Apistogramma reitzigi*
Yellow Dwarf Cichlid
Male 5–6 cm (2–2¼ in.), female 3·5 cm (1⅓ in.). Central part of the Rio Paraguay. The colour pattern is very variable and depends upon the temperature. For care and breeding see the description of the genus.

257. *Apistogramma trifasciatum haraldschultzi*
Male 5 cm (2 in.), female 3·5 cm (1⅓ in.). Upper Rio Guapore and Mato Grosso. A very attractive fish, but not often imported. For care and breeding see the description of the genus.

258. *Apistogramma wickleri*
Male 8 cm (3 in.), female 4 cm (1½ in.). Range not known in detail. For care, see generic description.

259. *Astronotus ocellatus*
35 cm (13¾ in.); in the home aquarium up to 25 cm (9¾ in.). Widely distributed in large rivers in tropical South America. The illustration shows a natural-size young specimen. These cichlids should be kept in very large tanks. They are peaceful fishes, whose only drawback is that they grow too large. They are best kept in tanks without plants as they like to dig. Water type not critical. Temperature: 24–27°C (75–81°F). Omnivorous and very voracious, these are typical open-spawning, monogamous fish, which lay up to 700–800 eggs at a time.

Cichlasoma
A South American genus containing medium-sized to large typical open-spawning, often very aggressive cich-

lids. They should be kept in large, unplanted tanks with firmly fixed rocks or old roots. The species described here will thrive in ordinary tap water at temperatures around 25°C (77°F). Most species are omnivorous but the main part of their diet should consist of meat. They are incredibly voracious with a fast digestion, so there should be frequent changes of a quarter of the tank water. Most of the species are too aggressive for more than a single adult pair to be kept in a large tank. They are essentially monogamous and a good pair will remain mated for life. Few problems should be encountered in breeding these cichlids, except that it may be difficult to dispose of the numerous offspring; besides a large brood of young requires enormous quantities of food.

260. *Cichlasoma octofasciatum* [*Cichlasoma biocellatum*]
Jack Dempsey
18 cm (7 in.), but rarely more than 12–15 cm (4¾–6 in.) in the aquarium. Central Amazon region, Rio Negro. Sex differences: female paler with more rounded fins than the male, and sometimes a little smaller. An attractive but very aggressive cichlid; the female lays up to 700–800 eggs at a time.

261. *Cichlasoma citrinellum*
35 cm (13¾ in.). Distribution not known with certainty. Sex difference: at an age of 2 years the adult males develop a highly arched forehead. The young are an inconspicuous brown or ochre colour. The brilliant red colour is only developed at an age of 1½–2 years and with good feeding. Adult specimens are very aggressive, but suitable breeding pairs can be obtained by rearing 6–10 young in a large tank and allowing them to form

their own pairs. The female lays up to 1,000 eggs.

262. *Cichlasoma festivum*
Festivum

15 cm (6 in.). Amazon and western Guyana. A peaceful cichlid which in the wild lives in small shoals, often together with angelfishes. There are no external sex differences, except at spawning time when the female has a thick stumpy ovipositor while the male has a pointed and somewhat slender genital papilla. This species is reckoned to be difficult to breed, partly because it is not easy to find suitable pairs and partly because the eggs often go mouldy. A varied diet of live food is essential for successful breeding. The eggs are laid on the upperside of broad leaves and at a temperature of 27°C (81°F) they hatch in about 2 days. The young are free-swimming after hanging from a leaf for a further 2 days. They are not difficult to rear. See also No. 271.

263. *Cichlasoma meeki*
Firemouth Cichlid

15 cm (6 in.). Guatemala and Yucatan. Sex differences: female paler than the male and with the tips of the dorsal and anal fins more rounded. This species is usually very peaceful, except during the breeding periods, and it does not dig so actively as other species of *Cichlasoma*. Care and breeding as given in the description of the genus. *Cichlasoma meeki* can be crossed with No. 264 but the offspring are sterile.

264. *Cichlasoma nigrofasciatum*
Zebra Cichlid

15 cm (6 in.), but rarely more than 10 cm (3¾ in.) in the home aquarium. Lakes Atitlan and Amatitlan in Guatemala. Sex difference: male

more brightly coloured than female at spawning time. An incredibly restless and aggressive cichlid, both towards other members of its own species and to other fishes. It should be kept in a large aquarium tank (100–150 litres, 21–39 U.S. gals).

265. *Cichlasoma spilurum*

Male 10 cm (3¾ in.), female 8 cm (3 in.). Guatemala. Sex differences: male larger than the female, with a more domed forehead and more pointed dorsal and anal fins. A peaceful fish, which differs from the other species of *Cichlasoma* in that the eggs are laid in cavities; in the aquarium it will spawn in flowerpots. In other respects care and breeding are as described under the genus.

266. *Crenicara filamentosa*

Male 9 cm (3½ in.), female 4·5 cm (1¾ in.). Central Amazon region. Sex differences: female paler, smaller and with more rounded fins than the male. Care and breeding as given for the genus *Apistogramma*, page 195. This is regarded as one of the most difficult of the dwarf cichlids, and not without reason, for it is very susceptible to disease. Most of the successful breeding results have been attained when the water has been soft and acid with good circulation. The female seldom lays more than 100 eggs at a time.

267. *Geophagus jurupari*

25 cm (9¾ in.), but rarely more than 18 cm (7 in.) in the home aquarium. North-east Brazil and Guyana. No obvious sex differences. These fish and related species feed by taking mouthfuls of sand into the large mouth, chewing it, sifting out the edible particles and ejecting the sand through the gill slits. In an

aquarium tank they will keep the bottom clean for a depth of an inch or two.

The species of *Geophagus* are often very shy and they should be kept in a large, quiet tank with hollow tree roots or small caves to provide hiding-places. Most of them thrive in any type of well-circulated water at a temperature of *c*. 26–27°C (79–81°F). The diet should be mainly live: *Tubifex*, gnat larvae and *Daphnia*, but they will also take dead food. The adults may be somewhat aggressive towards one another, but by and large they are peaceful and should not be kept together with other more voracious cichlids, as they are easily chased away from their food.

The eggs are laid as in open-spawning cichlids, but the newly hatched young are taken into the mouth, according to several accounts by both the male and female, and there they spend their larval life. There are only scattered observations on breeding which is evidently difficult. On the other hand, the young are not very difficult to rear.

268. *Apistogramma ramirezi*
[*Microgeophagus ramirezi*]
Ramirez's Dwarf Cichlid

Male 7 cm (2¾ in.), female somewhat smaller. Venezuela, Bolivia and the Santa Cruz region. One of the most attractive dwarf cichlids which on account of inadequate selection of aquarium stocks has unfortunately become much reduced in size in comparison with the specimens originally imported. This species should be kept and bred under the conditions described for the genus *Apistogramma*, except that it likes a somewhat higher temperature, *c*. 28°C (82°F), and good water circulation. There is a certain amount of uncertainty about its systematic position. In its breeding

behaviour it differs from the species of *Apistogramma* in that it is monogamous, spawns in the open and shows no sexual dimorphism. Nowadays it is only rarely that this cichlid breeds naturally in the aquarium as the parent fish usually eat the eggs before they hatch. The eggs therefore have to be hatched artifically. The fry can be fed at first on *Artemia* nauplii. The female lays up to 250 eggs. This species occurs as a golden and as a completely white form.

269. *Nannacara anomala*
Golden-eyed Dwarf Cichlid

Male 8 cm (3 in.), female 6 cm (2¼ in.). Western Guyana. Sex differences: female smaller and with more rounded fins than male, and the flanks of the male show more green iridescence than those of the female. The illustration shows a female in breeding dress; at other times the female has a clay or ochre colour. Care and breeding as for No. 253.

270. *Nannacara taenia*
Lattice Dwarf Cichlid

Male 5 cm (2 in.), female 3·5 cm (1⅜ in.). Distinguished from No. 269 by its smaller size, and also by the more slender body and more pointed head of the male. Both these species of *Nannacara* are very variable in colour and pattern.

271. *Pterophyllum scalare*
Angelfish

Up to 15 cm (6 in.) long, and almost twice as tall. Along the banks of the Amazon and Rio Negro, and tributaries.

At one time *Pterophyllum scalare* was thought to be different from *P. eimekei*, but the latter is now regarded as a synonym of the former. The genus also includes the slightly smaller *P. altum* from the Orinoco, in which the body is even taller in relation to the length, and there is possibly a third species, *P. dumerilii*.

Since *P. scalare* was first introduced to the aquarium world in 1909 it has become extremely popular and widespread. This has resulted in a series of more or less successful selected forms such as the Veiltail Angel and the Black Angel and others with different spotted patterns. These strains have been crossed indiscriminately with one another and with the original form, so that nowadays one rarely sees really good specimens of the original Angelfish.

These fish should be kept in a large, tall tank (depth 50 cm (20 in.) or more) with plenty of plants such as *Echinodorus* and *Vallisneria*. The water should be slightly acid at a temperature of 24–27°C (75–81°F), and must be free of suspended detritus and bacteria. If they are really to thrive they should be given a varied diet of live food: gnat larvae, *Daphnia, Tubifex*, small earthworms and occasionally whiteworms. One of the reasons so many young Angelfish are sold is that they quickly die off because they are kept in tanks that are too small and are given an insufficient amount of live food.

A well-matched pair can be obtained by keeping a small group of the young and letting them choose their own mates. They are typical 'open-spawners', the eggs being laid on the upper surface of large leaves. Unfortunately, in the aquarium the young are seldom reared naturally, because they are often eaten by their parents. If natural rearing is to be successful the tank should be large with plenty of vegetation, and it must be sited in a quiet place, as Angelfish have a tendency to panic when disturbed.

Artificial hatching can be achieved by transferring the leaf with the eggs (keeping it under water) to a small glass tank where it is anchored vertically. A filter should have been fitted beforehand, and it is obvious that the water must be of the same type as that in the parent's tank. The leaf should be positioned below the outflow of the filter. One can also use a weak solution (pale blue) of methylene blue to prevent the eggs being attacked by bacteria and fungi.

The rearing of the young is not particularly difficult. The illustration shows young in various stages: (*a*) newly hatched at twice natural size, (*b*) 14 days old at natural size, (*c*) 4–6 weeks old, natural size, (*d*) 8–10 weeks old, natural size and (*e*) about 6 months old.

It is interesting to note that when defending a territory the males emit loud creaking sounds.

Symphysodon
Discus Fishes
This genus probably contains only two valid species, *Symphysodon aequifasciata* with several subspecies and varieties, and *S. discus*. In nature discus fishes live in small groups or pairs in rivers and streams. Although they have now been kept and bred in the aquarium for some years it has never been possible to acclimatise them to ordinary hard tap water. They only thrive in water of the rainforest type with frequent changes of about half the volume of the tank (many breeders recommend a change of this type every week or fortnight). Temperature: 28–30°C (82–86°F). The tank should be set up as described under No. 271. It is important that it should be undisturbed. Flat, calcium-free rocks or pieces of slate, set vertically, will provide shelter for the fish. The lighting should be subdued. Many of these fishes have a tendency

to panic and they may then damage themselves. This applies particularly to wild-caught specimens and to those which have been moved from tank to tank. The diet should be as varied as possible, for if it is too monotonous some individuals will go on 'hunger strike'. The best foods are gnat and other insect larvae, and *Tubifex* can also be used provided it is well washed to avoid intestinal infections. Whiteworms should only be given for short periods. Aquarium stocks of discus can become accustomed to taking dead food.

A plentiful supply of food and good water hygiene are essential prerequisites for successful breeding. Suitable breeding pairs can only be obtained by keeping a number of fish together and letting them find their own mates. There are no reliable external sex differences. The sexes can only be distinguished at spawning time or just before, when one can see the female's short, conical ovipositor and the male's more pointed genital papilla. The eggs are laid on vertical rocks or on broad leaves which have previously been thoroughly cleaned. Discus are typical 'open-spawning' cichlids and in general they care for their young in the same way as other fishes in this family. There is, however, one exception. The eggs hatch in 2–3 days and after hanging from a rock or leaf for a further 4–5 days the larvae enter a critical period, during which they are completely dependent upon a secretion produced by the parents' skin. The young actually feed on this secretion, and its formation is dependent upon the water and dietary conditions already mentioned. The longer the young can feed on this nutritive mucus the better they thrive. After 10–12 days they can be given *Artemia* nauplii, and they should only be removed from the breeding tank

when they no longer show any interest in the parent fish, or vice versa. At an age of 3 months they will have acquired the typical circular shape, but the full coloration only appears after 8–9 months. Discus are attacked mainly by intestinal infections (often introduced in unwashed food) and by *Octomitus* (a microscopic flagellate protozoan).

272. *Symphysodon discus*
Discus
15 cm (6 in.). Central Amazon, Rio Negro and Rio Xingu. This species is considered to be more difficult to keep than Nos. 273 and 274.

273. *Symphysodon aequifasciata axelrodi*
Brown Discus
15 cm (16 in.). Amazon, Rio Urubu. This is the form most commonly kept and bred.

274. *Symphysodon aequifasciata haraldi*
Blue Discus
15 cm (6 in.). Amazon (Leticia, Benjamin Constant). There are several strains of this form, which vary in their geographical distribution and in the intensity of the wavy blue lines.

There is also the Green Discus, *S. aequifasciata aequifasciata*.

275. *Etroplus maculatus*
Orange Chromide
8 cm (3 in.). India and Sri Lanka. Occurs in brackish as well as fresh waters. No reliable external sex difference. A typical 'open-spawning' cichlid which should preferably be fed on live food. Temperature: 25–28°C (77–82°F).

276. *Haplochromis burtoni*
10 cm (3¾ in.). Eastern and central parts of Africa. Sex differences: the

male is more brightly coloured than the female and has 5–7 orange egg-spots with black borders on the anal fin. Egg-spots are found in the males of most mouth-brooding cichlids (and also in the females of many species) and they serve as signals during mating. When spawning the female lays very large eggs which she immediately takes into her mouth. By special swimming movements the male shows off the egg-spots on his anal fin in front of the female. She takes them to be eggs which she has not collected and tries to take them into her mouth. In doing so she touches the male's anal fin and this stimulates him to shed sperms which then fertilise the eggs in the female's mouth.

Haplochromis burtoni should be kept as described for the genus *Cichlasoma*. This is a voracious and very aggressive fish. At 25°C (77°F) the young take about 14 days to reach the free-swimming stage.

277. *Hemichromis bimaculatus*
   Jewel Cichlid
   [Red Cichlid]
15 cm (6 in.). Niger, Nile and Zaïre. Sex differences not apparent except during the breeding period when the female is more brightly coloured than the male. A very aggressive species which should be kept and bred as described for *Cichlasoma*, page 196.

278. *Hemihaplochromis multicolor*
   Egyptian Mouthbrooder
7 cm (2¾ in.). Large areas of eastern Africa. The male has no egg-spots in the anal fin, but the purple-red tip of this fin evidently serves the same function. Very easy to keep and breed.

Breeding starts when the brilliantly coloured male digs a pit in the bottom. At intervals the digging is interrupted and the male tries partly to chase, partly to entice a ripe female over the pit. When he has succeeded in doing this he assumes an S-shape and with gill-covers spread and fins held close to his body he tries to push the female round the periphery of the pit. If she is ready to spawn the pair glide slowly round with the pit as the central point. As they do so the female lays her eggs, a few at a time, and collects them in her mouth where they are fertilised as described under No. 276. At 25°C (77°F) the young are free-swimming in about 13 days.

279. *Nanochromis nudiceps*
   [*Nannochromis nudiceps*]
Male 8 cm (3 in.), female 6 cm (2¼ in.). River Zaïre. A sexually dimorphic species which spawns in cavities. The female is smaller and more attractively coloured than the male. The females often extrude the ovipositor long before the actual spawning. The eggs are laid in clusters on the roof of a cavity and are guarded by the female only. The males may be very aggressive and it is best to keep several females with a single male. This species is not very easy to breed. The female often takes the initiative, taking up a characteristic position with her body bent in an S-shape, see the lowermost illustration. There may be up to 100 young in a brood, and these are not difficult to rear.

Pelmatochromis and Pelvicachromis
The systematics of these West African cichlids is under constant revision and many of the scientific names have changed in recent years. From the aquarium viewpoint they are interesting and often very brightly coloured fishes, which can be kept in the

manner described under the genus *Apistogramma*, page 195. Most of the species will breed in ordinary hard tap water. In nature they live in estuaries or in other. often brackish waters near the coasts. In some cases, therefore, the addition of salt can be recommended.

280. *Thysia ansorgii*
[*Pelmatochromis ansorgei*]
Male 13 cm (5 in.), female 10 cm (3¾ in.). Coastal forest areas in Nigeria, Ghana and Ivory Coast. Sex differences: female smaller, paler and with more rounded fins than the male. A peaceful species which likes temperatures around 27°C (81°F). Broods up to 1,000.

The eggs are laid in holes or rock crevices and guarded often by both parents which also tend the young when they have become free-swimming. From the viewpoint of behaviour this and the following three species are intermediate between those cichlids that spawn out in the open and those that hide their eggs. The young are not difficult to rear.

281. *Chromidotilapia guntheri*
[*Pelmatochromis guentheri*]
Male 20 cm (7¾ in.), female 16 cm (6¼ in.), but seldom more than 15 cm (6 in.) in the aquarium. Forest and savanna areas from Ghana to Cameroun. Sex difference: female often more brightly coloured than male. This is an atypical mouth-brooder, for it is monogamous and almost without sexual dimorphism; the eggs are laid in holes but are taken into the mouth of the male. The young are free-swimming after some 14 days and are then tended by both parents. At this period they may be taken into the mouth of either parent. Broods up to about 200. This is one of the most aggressive species within the

group. Further breeding information as for No. 280.

282. *Pelmatochromis thomasi*
Male 7 cm (2¾ in.), female 6 cm (2¼ in.). Sierra Leone. No clear sex differences. A peaceful, 'open-spawning' cichlid which can be kept like No. 268. Broods up to 500. Further breeding information as for No. 280.

283. *Pelvicachromis pulcher*
(formerly *Pelmatochromis kribensis*)
Male 9 cm (3½ in.), female 7 cm (2¾ in.). Nigeria. A hardy, brightly coloured species in which the female lays up to 300 eggs in holes or rock crevices. The eggs and young are usually guarded by both parents or by the female alone. Further breeding information as for No. 280.

284. *Steatocranus casuarius*
African Blockhead
Male 10 cm (3¾ in.), female 7 cm (2¾ in.). Lower and Middle Zaïre, in fast-running streams. The male only has the dome-shaped fatty outgrowth on the head, and its dorsal and anal fins are more pointed and produced than those of the female. This is an omnivorous bottom-living cichlid with an incompletely developed swim-bladder. It should be kept in clear water that is kept moving and at a temperature of 24–26°C (75–79°F). The female lays up to 100 large, orange eggs in crevices and guards both these and young; one writer says that they are mainly guarded by the male. The female (? or male) masticates food for the tiny young. The young soon become territorial, probably because unlike most other cichlid fry they cannot swim in a shoal, owing to the poorly developed swimbladder. The young can be

reared in the same tank as the parents, which will not chase them, provided there are plenty of hiding-places.

Lake Malawi Cichlids

This is a very large group of cichlids which first started to appear in the aquarium world at the beginning of the 1960s. The situation of the large Lake Malawi (formerly Lake Nyasa), its isolation from other water masses and the presence of special ecological conditions have resulted in the evolution of a very characteristic fish fauna. This is dominated by the cichlids, which are classified in approximately 24 genera and over 200 species. Of these, all but a handful are endemic, that is, they only occur in Lake Malawi. Why so many different species have developed is still not fully understood, but the process may have been influenced partly by the great geological age of the lake and partly by the presence of a variety of different habitats, such as rocky coasts, open water, shallow sandy areas and so on. Although the lake extends down to a depth of 1,470 metres (4,800 feet) there is no true deep-water fauna below 125 metres (410 feet) because of the presence of sulphuretted hydrogen and the absence of oxygen. For the aquarium the most popular of these lake cichlids are the brightly coloured species in the genera *Labeotropheus, Labidochromis* and *Pseudotropheus*, and to a lesser extent the *Haplochromis* species from the open water and the areas with a sandy or rocky bottom.

The fact that the Malawi cichlids require fairly hard, alkaline water renders them well suited as aquarium fishes in areas with hard tap water, which can be used directly for replenishing and renewing the tank water. Plants cannot really be kept in a tank with these cichlids. The build-up of nitrate in the water can only be held in check by changing about one-third of the water, say, every third week.

Tanks to hold the species from rocky areas should have rockwork that offers as many hiding-places as possible. The water should be kept moving by a circulation pump and at a temperature of 24–27°C (75–81°F). Although many species are specialised for browsing on algal growths, all the known species will thrive on more or less any kind of live or dead food, provided there is a certain amount of vegetable matter.

Most of the species, and particularly the males, are rather aggressive towards one another. The pattern of aggressive behaviour can to a certain extent be disrupted by keeping several species and individuals together. At the same time one should always try to have three or four times as many females as males of a given species.

All the known Malawi cichlids are mouth-brooders and most are not difficult to breed. Spawning will take place in the ordinary tank in the typical mouth-brooder fashion, see Nos. 276 and 278, and sometimes in holes. The eggs are brooded in the female's mouth for 2–4 weeks. The brood may consist of just a few eggs or up to 50–60, depending upon the species and the size of the female. After spawning has ceased many aquarists transfer the mouth-brooding female to a small tank with a spacious cavern. Care is essential when catching up the female who must not be out of the water for more than a few seconds; it is really better to transfer her in a vessel of water. By the time they leave the female the young are quite large and can immediately take small *Cyclops*.

At first they remain hidden among the rocks and in crevices. In general, the Malawi cichlids are very resistant to most diseases.

285. *Labeotropheus fuelleborni*
14 cm (5½ in.). From rocky shorelines. Like certain other Malawi cichlids this species exhibits polymorphism; in this case there are two different types of female. The one shown in the illustration is marbled brown and orange and known as the OB form (orange blotch). The other female colour phase resembles the male but is usually somewhat paler. The presence of egg-spots on the anal fin is not a sex-distinguishing character, but these are usually larger and more brightly coloured in the male. A large female may lay up to 60 eggs. At 28°C (82°F) the young are free-swimming after 19–25 days.

286. *Labeotropheus trewavasae*
12 cm (4¾ in.). From rocky shorelines. Some females are marbled orange and black, see No. 285, but some are like the typical male, see the illustration. Occasional males are light blue marbled with black. During recent years an orange female phase marked with black and red dots has become popular among aquarists. As in the case of the other polymorphic Malawi cichlids the genetical basis for the several forms has not yet been elucidated. Young males are violet-blue, older males more whitish-blue. Breeding as for No. 285.

287. *Labidochromis vellicans*
9 cm (3½ in.). From rocky shorelines. A very attractive small species in which the male is usually a little larger than the female. The female lays up to 30 eggs, and the young are free-swimming after about 20 days.

288. *Melanochromis melanopterus*
   [*Melanochromis vermivorus*]
12 cm (4¾ in.). From rocky shorelines. Females are more brownish. A very aggressive species which should be kept as described on page 203. The female lays up to 40 eggs, and it is said that the young are free-swimming in 20–25 days.

289. *Pseudotropheus auratus*
12 cm (4¾ in.). From rocky shorelines. This was one of the first Malawi cichlids to be imported for aquarium purposes. For care, see page 203. The female lays up to 60 eggs, and at 26–27°C (79–81°F) the young should be free-swimming in 20–25 days. The young have the typical female pattern. Some of the males may be very aggressive.

290. *Pseudotropheus elongatus*
12 cm (4¾ in.). From rocky shorelines. Female more grey-blue than the male. A very aggressive species which can be kept as described on page 203. Up to 40 eggs in a brood, and the young are free-swimming after 20–25 days.

291. *Melanochromis vermivorus*
   [*Pseudotropheus fuscus*]
12 cm (4¾ in.). From rocky shorelines. The female is more greyish-white and brownish, whereas the male is black with longitudinal blue stripes. This is regarded by many as being one of the most aggressive species, and here it is particularly important to keep only one male with several females in a tank. Otherwise as for No. 289.

292. *Iodotropheus sprengerae*
   [*Pseudotropheus novemfasciatus*]
10 cm (3¾ in.). From Boadzulu island, which has a rocky shoreline. The colours of the male are more intense than those of the female. For care,

see page 203. A relatively peaceful species, in which the female lays up to 30 eggs. The young are free-swimming after about 24 days.

293. *Pseudotropheus tropheops*
10 cm (3¾ in.). From rocky shorelines. Dominant males may be almost blue-black. Care, as for the other Malawi cichlids. Brood up to 30 eggs. At a temperature of *c.* 26–27°C (79–81°F) the young are free-swimming after about 20 days. A very similar form is sold under the name *Pseudotropheus gracilior* but here as in many of the other Malawi cichlids there is still considerable confusion in the nomenclature. This is accentuated by the numerous colour phases and varieties.

294. *Pseudotropheus zebra*
16 cm (6¼ in.). From rocky shorelines. Several forms have been described under this name, and closer investigation may show that these are different species or that they represent a single species that is in the process of becoming split into a number of species. The position at the moment can be summarised as follows: 1) Males with black and pale blue stripes, a black throat and belly, and a variable number of yellow egg-spots on the hind part of the anal and dorsal fin, see No. 294b. The females of this form are ochre-yellow with black and orange markings. According to the size of the black markings these may be subdivided into a large-spotted and a small-spotted form; possibly there are also females that are uniform grey-blue. A striped male may become a uniform grey-brown colour when in an inferior social position. The ventral fins of the males are longer than those of the females. 2) Bright blue males (see No. 294a) with faint blue transverse stripes and a variable number of pale yellow egg-spots on the anal fin, more rarely also on the dorsal fin. The corresponding females are a uniform pale blue or violet-blue. Ventral fins again longer in the male than in the female. 3) Almost white males with white or whitish-grey females.

It is believed that these three types can interbreed, but that if they have a choice of mate they prefer one belonging to their own type or phase. In addition, males of different types are not so aggressive towards one another as are males of the same colour phase. In very recent years three other colour phases have been imported. One has a red dorsal fin, one is reddish-yellow and the third is a dwarf form. *Pseudotropheus zebra* can be kept like the other species, but on account of its size it needs a tank with a capacity of at least 250 litres (55 gallons). It is generally somewhat more difficult to breed than the others. The female lays up to 60 eggs, and at 27–28°C (81–82°F) the young are free-swimming after 21–30 days.

Lake Tanganyika Cichlids
The conditions in Lake Tanganyika are similar to those in Lake Malawi except that the water is harder, and the species named here (Nos. 295–301) can all be kept in the aquarium as described on page 203. About 200 cichlid species (in 38 genera) have so far been described from Lake Tanganyika and of these, 133 species (in 35 genera) are endemic.

295. *Tanganicodus irsacae*
[*Eretmodus cyanosticus*]
7 cm (2¾ in.). From rocky shorelines. Male somewhat bluer than female. This is a mouth-brooding species with eggs that are smaller than those of the Malawi cichlids.

296. *Julidochromis marlieri*

10–12 cm (3¾–4¾ in.). The sexes can only be distinguished by allowing young fish to sort themselves into pairs. This species should be kept in a spacious tank with numerous holes and other hiding-places. The eggs are laid on the roof of a cavity and are usually guarded by both parents. An adult breeding pair will spawn at intervals of a few weeks and the young from several broods are tolerated by the adults, which is somewhat exceptional among brood-protecting fishes. There is some uncertainty about the size of the broods but up to 190 in each have been described.

297. *Julidochromis ornatus*

8 cm (3 in.). In general, as for the preceding species, with which this one can be crossed, although the offspring are sterile.

In addition there are *Julidochromis regani* and *J. transcriptus* which can be kept as No. 296.

298. *Lamprologus congolensis*

15 cm (6 in.). River Zaïre. The male's flanks have shiny golden scales which are lacking in the female. According to Meinken the female, but not the male, has a dark eye-spot on the front part of the dorsal fin's soft rays. This is a very aggressive species in which the males establish harem colonies containing several smaller female territories. The eggs (50–80) are laid in cavities and guarded by the female only. At 25–26°C (77–79°F) they hatch in 11–13 days. The young are not difficult to rear.

299. *Lamprologus brichardi*

[*Lamprologus savoryi elongatus*]
8·5 cm (3¼ in.). The unpaired fins of the male are more pointed and produced than those of the female.

A very elegant fish with a body and fins more like those of a Paradise Fish than a cichlid. Care, as for No. 296. The female lays up to 300 eggs (diameter *c.* 1 mm, *c.* $\frac{1}{25}$ in.) in a cavity and these and the young are guarded by both parents. The young can be reared at first on *Artemia*. Brood-protecting fishes are exceedingly aggressive and should not be kept with other species.

300. *Tropheus duboisi*

8–10 cm (3–3¾ in.). From rocky shorelines. Sex difference: the female retains some of the juvenile's white or whitish-yellow markings on the back, whereas these disappear completely in adult males. Care, as given for Malawi cichlids, page 203. This is a mouth-brooding species in which the female lays 5–8 pea-sized eggs. These develop very slowly and at 25°C (77°F) it takes about 6 weeks before the young are free-swimming. According to a number of observers sexual maturity is not reached until the fish are about 2 years old. The illustration shows a young fish (left) and an adult male.

301. *Tropheus moorei*

10–12 cm (3¾–4¾ in.). From rocky shorelines. Sex differences: not obvious, but the male is somewhat brighter than the female. Care as for the preceding species, but this one is evidently more aggressive. Unlike other mouth-brooders the female lays her eggs in the open water and catches them before they reach the bottom. The 5–17 eggs are each *c.* 7 mm (*c.* ¼ in.) in diameter. At 24–25°C (75–77°F) development to the free-swimming stage takes about 6 weeks. The young (12–15 mm, *c.* ½ in.) are at first pale brown with 6–8 darker transverse stripes or they are completely dark brown.

Gobiidae
Gobies

A large family, in which most of the species are marine. They are mainly inconspicuously coloured bottom-living fishes which have not become widely distributed in the aquarium world. It is a characteristic of all the gobies that the ventral fins are fused to form a sucker. The species described here belong to the subfamilies Gobiinae (Nos. 302–304 and 307) and Periophthalminae or mudskippers (Nos. 305 and 306).

302. *Brachygobius aggregatus*
Bumblebee Fish

4·4 cm (1¾ in.). North Borneo and Philippines, in salt and brackish waters. For care, see No. 304.

303. *Brachygobius nunus*
Bumblebee Fish

4·2 cm (1½ in.). South-east Asia and the Greater Sunda Islands, in fresh and brackish waters.

304. *Brachygobius xanthozona*
Bumblebee Fish

4·5 cm (1¾ in.). Sumatra, Borneo and Java, in estuaries. Sex differences: the females are usually less brightly coloured than the males. Bumblebees are only suitable for a single species tank provided with numerous hiding-places in the form of rock crevices and small caves. They do best in brackish water (2 tablespoonfuls of sea salt in 10 litres (2½ U.S. gals) of hard tap water). They should be kept at 25–30°C (77–86°F) as they are very warmth-loving and can be fed on all kinds of live food. The 100–150 stalked eggs are laid in cavities (or flowerpots in the aquarium) and are guarded by the male. The young hatch in 4–5 days and are free-swimming from the start, when they can be fed on *Artemia* nauplii.

305. *Periophthalmus barbarus*
Mudskipper

15 cm (6 in.). From the Red Sea, East Africa and Madagascar to South-east Asia, Indonesia and northern Australia, in estuaries and mangrove swamps. The ventral fins are only fused at the base. This is a very variable species.

In nature, the mudskippers live in the tidal zone, spending most of their time out of the water. However, on account of their gill respiration they are dependent upon the water for keeping the gills wet (and also the skin). At low tide they live on the extensive mud banks which are then exposed and at high tide they move up the shore or onto the root systems of the mangroves. Adults are territorial and defend an area with a central vertical tunnel leading down into a system of burrows (*c.* 40 cm, 16 in. long), all dug by the male. They feed on crustaceans, worms, molluscs and insects which they catch with great dexterity.

In the aquarium, mudskippers can be kept in a large, shallow tank with a substrate of fine sand. The water need only be 50–75 mm (2–3 in.) deep, and there should be several roots and flat rocks to provide resting-places for the fish. They can be kept in pure fresh water, but they do much better in slightly brackish water. These are fascinating fish to watch and they can be accustomed to take almost all kinds of food, both live and dead. The temperature of the water and of the air above it should be kept at 25–29°C (77–84°F). Mudskippers have never bred in captivity.

306. *Periophthalmus koelreuteri*
[*Periophthalmus koelreutheri*]
Mudskipper

15 cm (6 in.). East Africa. The exact nomenclature of the species and

colour varieties of mudskippers is very difficult, but from the aquarium viewpoint they can all be treated in the same way, see No. 305.

307. *Stigmatogobius sadanundio*

8·5 cm (3¼ in.). Southern Asia, Great Sunda Islands and Philippines, in fresh water. Sex differences: female paler and with smaller fins than the male. Care, as given for Nos. 302–304, but no salt need be added. Never bred in the aquarium.

Anabantidae
Labyrinth Fishes

A family with numerous species, distributed in South-east Asia and tropical Africa (*Ctenopoma*). They are mostly small and often brilliantly coloured. The majority live in small, warm, organically polluted and therefore oxygen-deficient waters. As an adaptation to this they have evolved an accessory respiratory system, the labyrinth organ. This consists of much-folded lamellae, in the upper part of the gill chamber, covered with a thin layer of skin rich in blood vessels. Atmospheric air is taken in at the mouth and passed over this organ, where the oxygen in it is absorbed by the vascular epithelium. In this way these fishes are able to survive even in water that is very deficient in oxygen. The labyrinth organ only develops about 3–4 weeks after hatching and before this the young are entirely dependent upon gill respiration.

Labyrinth fishes thrive best in a tank with patches of dense vegetation reaching up to the surface in a few places. Ideally they should have soft, slightly acid water but many species do remarkably well in matured tap water filtered through sphagnum moss. In general, these are warmth-loving fishes, so the temperature should be kept at 25–29°C (77–84°F). Most species are predatory and do best on live food. In most species the males are very aggressive and in the breeding period so much so that females not ready to spawn or those which have just spawned will be chased and killed if they are not removed from the tank. All the species mentioned here practise some form of brood protection. A few labyrinth fishes are mouth-brooders but the majority are bubble-nest builders. The bubble-nest is built by the male, who secretes a tough mucus in his mouth which coats the bubbles of air that he spits out. It is possible that this secretion contains bactericidal and fungicidal substances. Fragments of plants may be incorporated in the structure and the whole nest is anchored to a leaf, tree root or similar object. Spawning begins by a male enticing a ripe female up under the nest. After a few sham matings the female starts to lay, often belly upwards with the male curled round her. In some species in which they contain oil the eggs rise on their own into the nest, in others the male collects them in his mouth and spits them into the nest, each one surrounded by a mucus-coated bubble of air. Labyrinth fishes are usually very prolific and broods of over 1,000 are not uncommon, e.g. in *Trichogaster* and others. After spawning has ceased the female is driven away and the male tends the nest until the eggs hatch in about 36 hours, and the young start to swim freely after a further 2–3 days. They should then be fed on very tiny live food (*Cyclops* and *Diaptomus* larvae, *Paramecium* and rotifers). After 8–10 days they can take newly hatched *Artemia* nauplii, and after 3–4 weeks the development of the labyrinth organ allows them to start breathing air. The water in the rearing tank should not be too deep, and the air temperature should be the same as that of the water (use a glass lid). In view of the large broods, care should be taken to change about one-third of the water very frequently. After the development of the labyrinth organ the young should not be difficult to rear.

The African labyrinth fishes are described under Nos. 318–323. The Asiatic species are under Nos. 308–317 and 324–331.

308. *Belontia signata*
Combtail

13 cm (5 in.). Sri Lanka. Sex differences: female paler than male, and lacking the much-elongated rays in the dorsal and anal fins. Care, as given under the family. Old specimens can be incredibly aggressive towards members of their own species and towards other fishes. This is a typical bubble-nest builder with brood care being undertaken by the male. There have, however, been records of cases in which both sexes took part in protecting both eggs and young. In some cases the period of brood protection extends beyond that which is normal in other species of labyrinth fish. The brood may be up to 100, and the eggs and young are rather large. The illustration shows a male (*above*) and a half-grown juvenile (*below*).

309. *Betta bellica*

11 cm (4¼ in.). Malay Peninsula, Perak State. Sex differences: male more brightly coloured than the female, and with more red in the caudal and anal fins. Care as given under the family. A bubble-nest builder.

310. *Betta splendens*
Siamese Fighting Fish

6 cm (2¼ in.). Malay Peninsula and Thailand. Sex differences: male more brilliantly coloured, slenderer and with more produced dorsal and anal fins than the female. The natural form, which is rarely imported, is very variable in appearance. It occurs in both clear and in highly polluted waters, and very commonly in paddy-fields, where it helps to reduce the number of mosquito larvae. The popular name of the species refers to the extremely aggressive behaviour of the males towards one another. Normally they are completely peaceful towards other species of fish. On the other hand, two males cannot tolerate the sight of one another and will immediately start a merciless lethal fight. In the East these fish have been used in contests, with two males placed together in a small glass container where they immediately start fighting.

Fighting Fish can be kept and bred as described under the family. The species builds a bubble-nest and broods of 400–500 are not uncommon. This is one of the hardiest aquarium fishes and it can tolerate temperatures below 20°C (68°F) for short periods. For breeding the temperature should be 25–29°C (77–84°F). The young, which are very tiny, should be fed like those of other labyrinth fishes: at first with extremely fine live food or with an artificial substitute for infusorians.

Fighting Fish show a great readiness to breed, a considerable degree of variation and a rapid rate of growth, and so it is not surprising that there are several domesticated races with much-elongated fins and very bright colours. Fighting Fishes with enormously developed fins are nowadays bred in large numbers and, like the Guppy, they are the subject of numerous competitions. In order to obtain the largest possible fin prolongations the males are removed from the brood as soon as they can be sexed (they have longer fins than the females). Each male is placed in a separate small glass container with 1–2 litres ($\frac{1}{4}$–$\frac{1}{2}$ gallon) of water, and so positioned that they can see one another throughout the whole period of growth. By constantly using threat behaviour involving the spreading of the fins and gill-covers the fins of the male develop to fantastic dimensions. The optimum development of the fins and coloration is achieved at an age of 5 months and most Fighting Fish do not live for more than a year.

311. *Colisa chuna*
Honey Gourami

4 cm ($1\frac{1}{2}$ in.). India, River Brahmaputra. Sex difference: female much paler than male. During the breeding period the ground colour of the female is greyish with a darker band running along the middle of each flank. Care and breeding as given on page 208. A bubble-nest builder.

312. *Colisa fasciata*
Giant Gourami

12 cm ($4\frac{3}{4}$ in.). Bengal, Burma, Thailand, Malay Peninsula. Sex differences: female duller than male, and with a more silvery belly. This species should be kept in a spacious tank. It breeds like the other labyrinth fishes that build bubble-nests, see page 208. The broods are often very large, with up to 1,000 eggs.

313. *Colisa labiosa*
Thick-lipped Gourami

8 cm (3 in.). Southern Burma. Sex differences: see the illustration. Care

and breeding as for the other bubble-nest builders in the family, see page 208.

314. *Colisa lalia*
Dwarf Gourami

5 cm (2 in.). India, in the Ganges, Jumna and Brahmaputra. Sex differences: see the illustration. Care and breeding as described under the family. This species has been observed to shoot down insects from plants above the water, in the manner of an archerfish. Several observers have also reported that the Dwarf Gourami can emit a growling sound during courtship and fights between rivals. This is probably characteristic of a number of labyrinth fishes.

315. *Macropodus concolor*

9 cm ($3\frac{1}{2}$ in.). Indo-China, in stationary and slow-flowing waters. According to Myers this is a subspecies of *Macropodus opercularis* (No. 317). Sex differences: male more brightly coloured and with more elongated unpaired fins.

316. *Macropodus cupanus dayi*
Brown Spike-tailed Paradisefish

7 cm ($2\frac{3}{4}$ in.). Malabar Coast, Burma and South Vietnam. Sex difference: unpaired fins more elongated in male than in female. This fish builds a large bubble-nest, sometimes in a cavity.

317. *Macropodus opercularis*
Paradisefish

9 cm ($3\frac{1}{2}$ in.). Korea, China, South Vietnam and Taiwan. Sex differences: male more brightly coloured and with the unpaired fins more elongated and pointed. This is believed to be the first tropical fish imported and bred in the Western World. It was imported into Europe as early

as the 1870s. This is one of the hardiest fishes, tolerating temperatures down to 15–16°C (59–61°F), although for breeding not below 23–24°C (73–75°F). The species should always be kept in a separate, densely planted tank, owing to the aggressive behaviour of the male during the breeding periods. A bubble-nest is built, and the brood may have up to 1,000 eggs. The young grow very rapidly.

Ctenopoma
African Labyrinth Fishes
This genus contains a number of protectively coloured, rather aggressive and voracious labyrinth fishes which are only rarely imported and kept as aquarium fishes. They can be kept in large, shallow, densely planted tanks with sphagnum-filtered soft water at a temperature of 26–29°C (79–84°F). Most species live in running water, so the tank water should be kept moving. Rather little is known about the general biology of the *Ctenopoma* species. They are very prolific and the females lay up to 1,000 small eggs, in some species in a bubble-nest, in others at random below the surface. A few species are possibly mouth-brooders.

318. *Ctenopoma acutirostre*
Spotted Climbing Perch
15 cm (6 in.). Middle Zaïre. Sex differences: not described. This species has not been bred in the aquarium.

319. *Ctenopoma ansorgii*
[*Ctenopoma ansorgei*]
7 cm (2¾ in.). West Africa, River Chiloango. Sex difference: male more intensely coloured than female. A bubble-nest builder, and one of the most peaceful species in the genus. For care, see the generic description.

320. *Ctenopoma congicum*
Congo Climbing Perch
9 cm (3½ in.). Lower Zaïre, Chiloango and Ubangi. Sex differences: male with taller body and longer ventral fins than female. A bubble-nest builder, in which spawning extends over a period of several days. Care and breeding not difficult.

321. *Ctenopoma fasciolatum*
Banded Climbing Perch
8 cm (3 in.). Zaïre basin. Sex differences: male more brightly coloured and with the unpaired fins more pointed and produced than in the female. This is the mostly commonly imported and bred species. A bubble-nest builder in which the female lays up to 1,000 eggs.

322. *Ctenopoma nanum*
Dwarf Climbing Perch
7 cm (2¾ in.). South Cameroun and River Zaïre. Similar in appearance to the preceding and possibly only a subspecies of it. Sex difference: female usually smaller and scarcely so brightly coloured as the male. The bubble-nest is built by the male, and in spawning he curls round the female who is stationed below the nest. There are numerous matings, each producing about 20 eggs, with a final total of several hundreds.

323. *Ctenopoma ocellatum*
Eye-spot Climbing Perch
16 cm (6¼ in.). River Zaïre. In general, as for No. 318.

Asiatic Labyrinth Fishes (continued)

324. *Sphaerichthys osphromenoides*
Chocolate Gourami
6 cm (2¼ in.). Sumatra and Malay Peninsula. Sex difference: not really apparent, the female's dorsal fin

possibly more rounded than that of the male. An attractive species but very difficult to keep. Evidently it only thrives in completely soft, acid water at a temperature of 27–30°C (81–86°F). The tank should be densely planted, not too brightly lit, and the diet varied. The Chocolate Gourami is very susceptible to various ecto-parasites and diseases (tuberculosis) and very sensitive to the drugs used to combat these. This species should be in a position to build a bubble-nest or to practise brood protection, by mouth-brooding, depending upon whether it is living in stationary or flowing water. There have been records of it being kept successfully in water containing a small amount of sea salt. One of the problems in attempting to breed this fish is to get the females to develop mature eggs. It is therefore essential to feed them intensively on a varied diet, including small gnat or midge larvae and various non-aquatic insects such as fruit-flies and aphids.

325. *Trichogaster leerii*
[*Trichogaster leeri*]
Pearl Gourami
11 cm (4¼ in.). Malay Peninsula, Thailand, Sumatra and Borneo. Sex differences: male brighter and with much-elongated rays in the dorsal and anal fins. Temperature: 26–28°C (79–82°F). In general, they should be cared for as described under the bubble-nest building labyrinth fishes, page 208. Brood up to 1,000.

326. *Trichogaster microlepis*
Moonlight Gourami
15 cm (6 in.). Cambodia and Thailand. Sex difference: ventral fin filaments orange in the male, white in the female. A bubble-nest builder, and very prolific.

327. *Trichogaster trichopterus* '*sumatranus*'
[*Trichogaster trichopterus sumatranus*]
Blue Gourami
13 cm (5 in.). Possibly an aquarium mutant of the less brightly coloured Three-spot Gourami, *Trichogaster trichopterus trichopterus*. Sex differ-ence: dorsal fin more pointed in the male than in the female. A hardy and very prolific bubble-nest builder.

328. *Trichogaster trichopterus* '*cosby*'
A selected form of No. 327, often wrongly called 'crosby'.

329. *Trichopsis schalleri*
4 cm (1½ in.). Thailand in the Nam-Mun region. Sex differences: male's fins somewhat more pointed than those of the female, which is duller. This species should be kept on its own in a single species tank in view of its small size, but otherwise treated like the other bubble-nest builders. They emit growling sounds when spawning. Brood up to 100. A warmth-loving species to be kept at 27–29°C (81–84°F).

330. *Trichopsis pumilus*
Dwarf Gourami
3·5 cm (1⅓ in.). South Vietnam, Thailand and Sumatra. As for the preceding species, but thrives best in soft water. The female lays only a small number of eggs.

331. *Trichopsis vittatus*
Croaking Gourami
6·5 cm (2½ in.). Malay Peninsula, South Vietnam, Thailand and Indo-nesia. Sex differences: male more brightly coloured than female, and with a pointed, produced anal fin. Otherwise as for No. 329. When spawning both sexes emit growling or croaking sounds. Brood up to 200.

Luciocephalidae
Pike-heads

332. *Luciocephalus pulcher*
   Pike-head
18 cm (7 in.). Malay Peninsula,
Banka, Billiton, Sumatra and Borneo,
in flowing waters. This fish has an
accessory air-breathing organ but no
swimbladder. According to present
experience the species is very difficult
to keep. It apparently needs soft
water with good circulation and a
plentiful insect diet. It has never been
bred in the aquarium, but is possibly a
mouth-brooder.

Atherinidae
Silversides
This is a tropical marine family, of
which only a few species have become
adapted to living in fresh water. They
can be recognised by the two divided
dorsal fins, of which the front one is
the smaller, while the rear one often
has one or more much elongated soft
rays behind a single spiny ray. These
are shoaling fishes which thrive best
in hard, oxygen-rich water with a
good circulation.

333. *Bedotia geayi*
15 cm (6 in.). Madagascar, in flowing
waters. An attractive and hardy
shoaling fish which does best in a
large tank with plenty of open water
for swimming and frequent changes
of about a quarter of the volume.
Temperature: 24–26°C (75–79°F).
Spawning extends over several days
and the large eggs are laid close to the
surface among fine-leaved plants. The
very large young, which also remain
near the surface, are not attacked by
the adults. When feeding the young
with *Artemia* the water should be
kept in movement so that the nauplii
reach the surface. This species is easy
to breed.

334. *Melanotaenia maccullochi*
   Dwarf Rainbowfish
7 cm (2¾ in.). North-eastern Australia
in running fresh waters. Care and
breeding as for the preceding species.
Up to 300 eggs in a brood.

335. *Melanotaenia nigrans*
   Australian Red-tailed
   Rainbowfish
15 cm (6 in.). Eastern and southern
Australia, in fresh and brackish
waters. The male is more brightly
coloured and slenderer than the
female. Care and breeding as for No.
333.

336. *Telmatherina ladigesi*
   Celebes Sailfish
7 cm (2¾ in.). Celebes. Care as for No.
333, but this species is considerably
more sensitive to sudden changes in
the temperature and composition of
the water. This is essentially a hard-
water fish which should be kept at
22–25°C (72–77°F). The eggs are laid
among fine-leaved plants over a
period of several days and are usually
attacked by the adult fish. The fry,
which keep close to the surface,
should be fed on fine, live food; they
grow slowly.

Tetraodontidae
Pufferfishes
A tropical and subtropical family, of
which only a few species occur in
fresh water, the remainder in brackish
or sea water. The teeth are fused to
form a parrot-like beak with which
the pufferfishes can crush snails and
bivalves. Most species have a diverti-
culum of the gullet which can be filled
with air or water so that the fish takes
on a spherical appearance. Several
of the pufferfishes are poisonous,
producing a toxin in the gonads,
which is then stored in other parts of
the body.
   Pufferfishes swim by means of the

rapid movements of the pectoral fins, assisted by the dorsal and anal fins; they lack ventral fins. In spite of their rather ungainly appearance they can move through the water quite fast when frightened. Most species become too large for the private aquarium, but when young they are attractive in a brackish-water tank, where they should not be kept with other fishes, many of which have a habit of nibbling their fins. Most pufferfishes are omnivorous, with a preference for the flesh of snails and bivalves. Many are very susceptible to attack by fungi, which may be difficult to cure. Only a few species have been bred in the aquarium, and the reports on reproductive behaviour are very contradictory. In *Tetraodon cutcutia*, which has been bred in fresh water, the eggs (*c.* 200–300) are laid on a firm substrate. The eggs and the young, which are small and difficult to rear, are guarded by the male.

337. *Carinotetraodon somphongsi*
Male 8 cm (3 in.), female 6 cm (2¼ in.). Rivers in Thailand. Sex differences apart from size: the belly is reddish in the male, pale grey with dark markings in the female, and the dorsal fin is reddish in the male, transparent in the female. They are omnivorous and not difficult to keep in a well-planted tank with medium-hard water. Spawning is said to be very violent and the eggs are laid among the plants, particularly Java Moss. During spawning the male hangs on to the female with his jaws. The young have not yet been reared in captivity.

338. *Tetraodon fluviatilis*
Green pufferfish
20 cm (7¾ in.). From India to the Philippines in fresh and brackish waters. This species is often imported when quite small. Care, as given in the family description. There is no reliable account of breeding in the aquarium.

339. *Tetraodon palembangensis*
20 cm (7¾ in.). Thailand, Sumatra and Borneo, in fresh waters. A very aggressive species which can be kept in fresh or brackish water.

MARINE FISHES

Most of the marine fishes kept in home aquarium tanks come from areas of tropical coral reef, and with only a few exceptions this applies to the species here numbered 340–455. In such areas the water forms a very constant medium and it is therefore possible to lay down certain guidelines. Many of the difficulties encountered in keeping reef fishes are concerned with the maintenance of this constant environment. The de-

tails of this subject are beyond the scope of this book, but the reader is referred to the bibliography on page 237. The following general points should, however, be helpful.

The tank should have a capacity of not less than 100 litres (26½ U.S. gals), and should preferably be over 200 litres (53 U.S. gals). It is best made by gluing together five panes of glass (four sides and one for the bottom), using a silicone glue, which unlike most other materials is not attacked by sea water.

The water should be made up from a ready-made sea salt mixture. These salts should be dissolved in ordinary tap water in plastic containers kept for the purpose, with continuous aeration until they have all dissolved. The specific gravity, to be measured with a hydrometer, should be *c.* 1·025 and the pH should be in the range 8·2–8·4.

The substrate should consist of any kind of gravel that is free of metals. Silica sand, limestone chippings or coral sand (crushed coral) are all suitable. If the tank has no bottom filter the thickness of the substrate should not exceed 3–4 cm ($1\frac{1}{4}$–$1\frac{1}{2}$ in.), otherwise decomposition may occur. Wrasses and other fishes which spend the night partly buried are quite content with this depth of substrate.

Decorative material. Most aquarists use a foundation of some form of limestone on which they fix or rest the dried skeletons of corals. These must be previously cleaned in a solution of 1 part of hypochlorite to 4–5 parts of water; this releases any organic matter from the skeleton in a period of 24–48 hours. After this cleaning process the corals must be rinsed 6–8 times in fresh water. Mollusc shells used for decoration should be treated in the same way.

Lighting should be by means of fluorescent tubes. In tanks with a capacity of over 200 litres (53 U.S. gals) the ratio between wattage and volume (in litres) should be 1:2. In other words, a tank with a capacity of 300 litres (79 U.S. gals) should be lit by 150–160 watts or, say, three or four 40 watt tubes. These should be switched on for 10–12 hours per day. There must never be any contact between the sea water and the electrical installation.

Temperature should be kept at 26–27°C (79–81°F), using a thermostat. Small fluctuations are not injurious, but sudden changes of more than 2–3°C ($\frac{3}{4}$–$1\frac{1}{4}$°F) may be fatal.

Water movement. The majority of coral-reef fishes will only thrive if there is sufficient movement of water. This can be achieved by using a circulation pump designed for sea water, such as the Eheim. The hourly capacity of the pump (in litres per hours) should be two or three times the litre capacity of the tank, and a turnover of 4–6 times the tank's capacity per hour is not injurious. The importance of water movement is often underestimated by many aquarists.

Water hygiene. The amount of waste products (primarily nitrogenous) in the water will depend upon the number of fish kept in the tank. These waste products are broken down by bacteria, first to ammonia and then to nitrite and nitrate. If not removed in some way the concentration of nitrate will increase and it may become poisonous when it exceeds 400–500 mg per litre (per 1·05 U.S. qts). There are several methods of preventing the build-up of nitrate in the water: 1) by replacing approximately one-sixth of the water every 14 days (or one-third every month) with fresh salt water, 2) by having a plentiful growth of algae, which are thinned out from time to time; the nitrate is a plant nutrient, so it is removed by the algae, 3) by having a sufficient growth of denitrifying bacteria in some form of biological filter; these bacteria break down nitrate directly to nitrogen and oxygen. Most aquarists will probably prefer to use the first method as the other two require a considerable amount of technical experience.

Filtration. There are several different kinds of filter designed either to remove nitrogenous waste (ammonia, nitrite, nitrate) or merely to sieve out particulate matter. In a *bacterial* or *biological filter* the surface of the medium carries bacteria which are thus in contact with the polluted water and they break down nitrogenous substances to nitrate or to nitrogen and oxygen. In a bottom filter the tank substrate acts as the filter medium. In a *physical filter* the medium binds or adsorbs organic particles on its surface, as for example in an activated charcoal filter or in one with nylon wool which literally sieves particles from the water. To be effective such filters must be cleaned very frequently, every day or every second day. If they operate for longer periods without being cleaned they automatically become bacterial or biological filters. The foam filter or protein skimmer is in a rather special category; this is a relatively simple piece of apparatus in which a stream of fine bubbles blown up a tube collects the nitrogenous substances in the form of a scum or foam which can then be removed.

Aeration. The primary function of aeration is to keep the surface in motion so that the water can take up oxygen from the air. Aeration can also be used to operate a slow bottom filter.

Ozone (O_3) *and ultraviolet light.* The use of these is said by some aquarists to be beneficial. It is believed that ozone accelerates the precipitation of albuminoid substances during filtration. Ozonisation should always take place in an isolated filter chamber, as free ozone is injurious to fishes. Ultraviolet light destroys bacteria, both the beneficial and the injurious ones, and it can be shown that many injurious bacteria quickly develop a resistance to ultraviolet light.

Feeding. In nature many coral-reef fishes are essentially specialist feeders, but most of them can become accustomed to the types of food used in the freshwater aquarium. The text indicates where a species is difficult or impossible to keep on account of its special food requirements. Raw fish flesh and roe (from cod, herring, etc.) have proved useful foods for marine fishes. The usual live foods from fresh waters can also be used, but it should be remembered that these animals die very quickly in sea water. Newly hatched *Artemia* are taken by many species, and fairy shrimps (*Mysis*) can also be used by those aquarists who can catch them in coastal waters, mostly in July–November.

Canthigasteridae
A small family of marine pufferfishes which are rather similar in appearance and habits to Nos. 337–339.

340. *Canthigaster margaritatus*
15 cm (6 in.). Indo-Pacific. Sex differences: none known. An undemanding, omnivorous fish which may live for years, but like other pufferfishes it is very susceptible to fungal attacks which can be very difficult to cure. There is no record of breeding in the aquarium.

341. *Canthigaster valentini*
Up to 25 cm (9¾ in.), but seldom more than 10 cm (3¾ in.) in the aquarium. Indo-Pacific.

Lutjanidae U.S.A.
Lutianidae Britain
Snappers
A family of quite large fishes which live singly or in shoals in the vicinity of tropical coasts. In the aquarium they are hardy, omnivorous and fast-growing, and on account of their

voracity they should not be kept with small species.

342. *Lutjanus sebae*
    [*Lutianus sebae*]
    Emperor Snapper
c. 100 cm (39 in.), but rarely more than 30 cm (11¾ in.) in the aquarium. Coastal reefs from the Philippines to the Indo-Australian Archipelago. Only young specimens are suitable for a private aquarium.

Serranidae
Groupers
A family of approximately 400 species, mostly occurring in tropical and subtropical seas. The majority are solitary, voracious predators which live in submarine caves and rock crevices. Most are hardy and some may attain a great age in large aquaria. Biologically many are interesting as they are hermaphrodite. Only the smaller species are suitable for the home aquarium. The best-known genera are: *Cephalopholis, Chromileptis, Epinephelus, Grammistes, Mycteroperca, Serranellus,* and *Anthias*.

343. *Anthias squamipinnis*
10 cm (3¾ in.). Indo-Pacific, where they live in small shoals in or near caves and crevices. This is a rather variable species, in fact it is possible that there are five species. They can be difficult to keep in the aquarium, and only appear to thrive when kept in a small group of 5–8. Such a group is usually dominated by one individual, who develops elongated fins, particularly the caudal. Feeding can present difficulties, for in spite of its large mouth this fish prefers small live food, such as *Cyclops* and mosquito larvae, although it can also become accustomed to take cod's roe, finely chopped fish and prawn

flesh. They are best fed in dim light in the evening. *Anthias* is very sensitive to changes in the temperature and composition of the water.

Grammidae U.S.A.
Pseudochromidae Britain
A family of small, omnivorous, crevice-dwelling reef fishes with an elongated body. They live quite well in the aquarium once they have settled down.

344. *Gramma loreto*
8 cm (3 in.). Caribbean Sea, Bermuda and the West Indies, in submarine caves. Sex differences: male possibly somewhat larger and with longer fin filaments than the female. In the aquarium it lives hidden away for much of the time, and appears to swim with equal facility upside down. The male builds a nest of algae and other material in which the female lays up to 400 eggs. Both parents guard the eggs until they hatch but after this the brood disperses. There are no records of successful breeding in captivity. This species only does well if provided with good hiding-places. It is said to act as a cleaner, see No. 412.

Apogonidae
Cardinal Fishes
A family of small fishes that live singly or in groups in the vicinity of coral reefs or in quite shallow water. They are characterised in part by having two separate dorsal fins. They are rather stationary fishes and in the aquarium should not be kept together with species that are too aggressive. They thrive best in a small group and prefer small live food. The males are mostly smaller than the females, but with a larger head. After spawning the eggs are taken into the mouth of one of the parents, usually probably the male, where they are incubated.

The individual eggs have long filaments which help to keep them together in a mass. The species *Siphamia versicolor* and *S. zaribae* act as cleaners, living among the spines of the tropical sea-urchin *Diadema* and taking part of their food by cleaning its skin.

345. *Apogon nematopterus*
     Pyjama Cardinal Fish
8 cm (3 in.). From the Philippines to the Indo-Australian Archipelago. This species should be kept in a small tank, at least at first, and fed on small live food. It is not always easy to keep.

Holocentridae
Soldierfishes and Squirrelfishes
A large family of quite large, active, nocturnal fishes from tropical regions. During the day they remain hidden in caves and crevices. Most of the species have spines on the gill covers and on some of the fins. Only young specimens are suitable for the private aquarium. They are very voracious and so should only be kept with species of the same size as themselves.

346. *Holocentrus diadema*
     [*Holocentrus xantherythurus*]
25 cm (9¾ in.). Indo-Pacific. For care see the family description.

347. *Myripristis murdjan*
30 cm (11¾ in.). Indo-Pacific. The most commonly imported species, which should be kept as a group in a large tank.

Sciaenidae
Drums
A tropical family of fairly large, shoaling fishes which live near the coasts or in the vicinity of coral reefs. They can produce sounds, hence the popular name. This is done by the rapid vibration of special muscles in the region of the swimbladder. On account of their size drums are only suitable for a large tank, and they should be kept as a group. The two species described here are very popular in the U.S.A., but are only rarely imported into Europe. They mainly occur in the Atlantic Ocean and the Caribbean Sea.

348. *Equetes acuminatus*
     [*Eques acuminatus*]
     High-hat
     [Cubbyu]
30 cm (11¾ in.), but seldom more than 15 cm (6 in.) in the aquarium. Bermuda and South Carolina to Rio de Janeiro. Spawning has been described as violent with the female taking the initiative. The pair swims round in circles as the eggs are laid. Drums feed mainly on crustaceans.

349. *Equetes lanceolatus*
     [*Eques lanceolatus*]
     Jack-knife Fish
25 cm (8¾ in.). West Indies and Florida.

Pomadasyidae U.S.A.
Plectorhynchidae Britain
Sweetlips
A family of large fishes living near coral reefs and in shallow water. In many of them the colours of the juveniles and adults differ, and so the nomenclature is confused. They are only suitable for the aquarium when young. They prefer live food and plenty of space for swimming. Before buying these fishes it is advisable to make sure that they have been feeding, as they very often sicken without taking food at all. Their method of swimming resembles the bending and twisting of clownfishes. They are very sensitive to temperatures below 25–26°C (77–79°F).

350. *Plectorhynchus chaetodonoides*
45 cm (17¾ in.), but rarely more than 20 cm (8 in.) in the aquarium. Indo-Australian Archipelago. A rather difficult species that should be fed on live food, such as fairy shrimps and mosquito larvae, but it can be accustomed to take dead food. Temperature: 26–29°C (79–84°F).

Chaetodontidae
Butterflyfishes
A large family of coral-reef fishes with a tall laterally compressed body and a small mouth. They are specialised feeders which take coral polyps, tube-dwelling worms and other animals which they pick out of the corals. Many species live in pairs on the reefs and are very faithful and therefore aggressive. When young they often live socially in small groups. On account of their elegant and quite fantastic colours they are much sought after by marine aquarists. They are, however, not very hardy as aquarium fishes. With a few exceptions, it is probable that most of them do not live for long in private aquaria. They require clear, absolutely clean sea water, containing a minimum of nitrate, and with a good circulation. Specimens that survive the first 2–3 months in the aquarium and start to feed properly may live for years. Little is known about their breeding habits and none of the species have yet been bred in captivity. The most suitable species for the aquarium belong to the genera *Heniochus*, *Chelmon* and *Forcipiger*.

351. *Heniochus acuminatus*
Pennant Coralfish
25 cm (9¾ in.), but rarely more than c. 14 cm (5½ in.) in the aquarium. Widely distributed in the Indo-Pacific. Very young specimens may be delicate and difficult to get to feed;

otherwise these are very suitable fish for the aquarium, which thrive best and look most beautiful when kept as a small group. It usually becomes accustomed quite quickly to take the usual types of food.

352. *Chelmon rostratus*
Long-nosed Butterflyfish
17 cm (6¾ in.), but rarely more than c. 13 cm (5 in.) in the aquarium. Malay Archipelago to the Philippines. This must be regarded as a difficult fish for the aquarium, for it often refuses to feed. It is certainly not suitable for the inexperienced aquarist. It may become very aggressive towards its fellows.

353. *Forcipiger flavissimus*
20 cm (7¾ in.). From the Philippines to Sri Lanka. This is the species of *Forcipiger* most commonly imported, but in the past it has been wrongly called *F. longirostris*. The latter has an even longer snout with a smaller, more tubular mouth and only eleven dorsal fin rays, whereas *F. flavissimus* has twelve. The names *F. cyrano* and *F. inornatus* are synonyms of *F. longirostris*.

Zanclidae
354. *Zanclus canescens*
[*Zanclus cornutus*]
Moorish Idol
25 cm (9¾ in.). Indo-Pacific, where it lives in shoals of up to several hundreds on the coral reefs. Most specimens arrive at the importers in very bad condition and die of their injuries. It is, in fact, completely unsuitable as an aquarium fish, unless it can be kept in a tank with a capacity of over 1,000 litres (264 U.S. gals).

This species belongs to a family which only has a single genus. From the systematic viewpoint it can be regarded as intermediate between the families Chaetodontidae and Acanthuridae.

Chaetodontidae (continued)

355. *Chaetodon auriga*
Up to 18 cm (7 in.). Indo-Pacific and Red Sea. The illustration shows a young specimen in natural size. This is one of the hardiest of the *Chaetodon* species, but very aggressive towards its fellows.

356. *Chaetodon chrysurus*
15 cm (6 in.). Indo-Pacific and Red Sea, where it occurs in several local varieties. Otherwise as for No. 355.

357. *Chaetodon collaris*
[*Chaetodon collare*]
15 cm (6 in.). Indo-Pacific. In the opinion of many aquarists this is the most suitable *Chaetodon* species for the aquarium. It quickly becomes accustomed to taking fairy shrimps (*Mysis*), mosquito larvae, *Tubifex* and dead food.

358. *Chaetodon kleinii*
12 cm (4¾ in.). Indo-Pacific. A rarely imported species which normally starts to feed quite quickly.

359. *Chaetodon ephippium*
25 cm (9¾ in.). Indo-Pacific. This is one of the more delicate species and may be difficult to get to feed. As the illustration shows there is a big difference between juvenile and adult.

360. *Chaetodon larvatus*
9 cm (3½ in.). Red Sea. A rarely imported, difficult species.

361. *Chaetodon lunula*
18 cm (7 in.) Indo-Pacific, Australia and Hawaii. One of the best species for the aquarium. Normally it starts to take a variety of food quite quickly.

362. *Chaetodon melannotus*
[*Chaetodon melanotus*]
16 cm (6¼ in.). Red sea and large areas of the Indo-Pacific. Often imported but a difficult species for the aquarium. The illustration shows a young specimen in natural size.

363. *Chaetodon ocellatus*
Spotfin Butterflyfish
14 cm (5½ in.). West Indies and the coasts of Florida. Compared with many other species in the genus this is a very hardy fish in the aquarium.

364. *Chaetodon ornatissimus*
17 cm (6¾ in.). Indo-Pacific and Hawaii. According to many authors it is very difficult to persuade this species to feed.

365. *Chaetodon xanthocephalus*
20 cm (7¾ in.). Indo-Pacific. A very attractive but difficult species. The illustration shows a young specimen, natural size.

Pomacanthidae
Marine Angelfishes
A family of stately, beautifully coloured fishes from tropical seas, but mostly from the Indo-Pacific. They are characterised by a backward directed, knife-like spine on the lower part of the gill cover, which is lacking in the closely related family Chaetodontidae. In nature, these fishes live in pairs or in shoals. They feed principally on plant food and small crustaceans, which they 'graze' from the substrate. Many species pass through various different colour phases between the juvenile and the adult, and most have reached their adult colour phase when they are 8–9 cm (3–3½ in.) long. Apart from the dwarf species in the genus *Centropyge* most of the marine angelfishes become too large for the private aquarium, and they are all very

aggressive towards other members of their own species. Most can be accustomed to taking the usual aquarium foods, but care should be taken that all foods, dead or live, are offered in small pieces. One should not be misled by their very large and fierce-looking mouths.

The best method of acclimatising marine angelfishes is to put them in a tank with plenty of algal growth, and so far as possible to keep the algae growing. Other good foods are newly hatched *Artemia*, small *Mysis*, *Cyclops* and chopped *Tubifex* or small earthworms. Once they are acclimatised they may live for years and are not particularly sensitive to disease or to drugs, provided they are not over *c*. 8–9 cm (3–3½ in.) on arrival. They have favourite hiding-places in the tank, usually spacious cavities or crevices in the rockwork, in which they will remain for long periods at a time. None of the species has been bred in the aquarium and there are no known external sex differences.

366. *Chaetodontoplus mesoleucus*
15 cm (6 in). Indo-Pacific. As the generic name implies this fish is somewhat similar to *Chaetodon*. On closer examination, however, it can be seen to have the form typical of the marine angelfishes, with a gill-cover spine. A difficult fish to acclimatise in the aquarium.

367. *Pomacanthus annularis*
40 cm (15¾ in.). Indo-Pacific. The juvenile stages of this and the following two species are rather similar, but the adults differ widely. For care, see the family description.

368. *Pomacanthus semicirculatus* (young)
40 cm (15¾ in.). Indo-Pacific. In the adults the body is yellowish with dark markings, the head black with white lips and the unpaired fins blue-black with small white dots. For care, see the family description.

369. *Pomacanthus imperator*
Imperial Angelfish
36 cm (14 in.). Indo-Pacific. One of the most sought-after of all the coral-reef fishes, but because of its size not really suitable for the home aquarium.

370. *Pomacanthus arcuatus* (young)
French Angelfish
40 cm (15¾ in.). West Indies, north to New Jersey and south to Bahia. The juvenile pattern is similar to that of *Pomacanthus paru*, but in *P. arcuatus* the central yellow band ends roughly in the middle of the dorsal fin, whereas in *P. paru* it extends out to the tip of this fin. In *P. arcuatus* the caudal fin has a broad, almost perpendicular yellow band at the base, followed by a narrow half-moon shaped black marking and then a broad, un-coloured fin border. In *P. paru* the caudal fin is dominated by a large oval, black marking, in front of which is a narrow, curved, yellow band which joins the caudal fin border to form a ring. This is a difficult species to keep.

371. *Pomacanthus paru* (young)
40 cm (15¾ in.). Tropical Atlantic Ocean. When adult this species is blackish-violet with yellow scale edges, yellow 'spectacles' and a yellow spot at the base of each pectoral fin, and is thus distinguished from the uniform, grey-black *P. arcuatus* (see preceding species).

372. *Holacanthus tricolor*
Rock Beauty
60 cm (23 in.). Tropical Atlantic Ocean, Caribbean Sea. This is a beautiful but rather delicate fish. For

care, see the family description. The young have a circular, black marking on the rear, uppermost part of the body. With increasing age this marking extends over the whole rear part of the body and out on to the dorsal and anal fins.

373. Pygoplites diacanthus
20 cm (7¾ in.). Indo-Pacific and Red Sea, on coastal reefs. A very delicate fish, rarely imported, which requires plenty of hiding-places. See also the family description.

374. Euxiphipops navarchus
30 cm (11¾ in.). Indo-Australian Archipelago. One of the most beautiful of the marine angelfishes, but it may be difficult to acclimatise. For care, see the family description.

375. Euxiphipops xanthometopon
30 cm (11¾ in.). Indo-Australian Archipelago. Like the preceding species this is a difficult fish and it should therefore only be kept by very experienced aquarists who can give it proper quarters and a sufficiently varied diet.

376. Centropyge bispinosus
12 cm (4¾ in.). Indo-Pacific. This and the following three species are, on account of their size, more rewarding as aquarium fishes than the larger members of the family. Centropyge bispinosus is one of the hardiest and there are rarely any problems in getting it to feed.

377. Centropyge fisheri
8 cm (3 in.). Indo-Pacific. Once acclimatised this is a very hardy form, which feeds extensively on algae.

378. Centropyge flavissimus
10 cm (3¾ in.). Central Pacific. Sometimes confused with Centropyge heraldi, which has no blue markings.

379. Centropyge tibicen
13 cm (5 in.). East Indies, Philippines and Melanesia.

Pomacentridae
Damselfishes
A large family of tropical fishes, found on coral reefs, and also in certain subtropical waters. Their closest relatives in fresh water may be the cichlids. The family contains some of the most suitable fishes for the marine aquarium, both as regards beauty and hardiness. Some of the species in the genera Abudefduf, Chromis, Dascyllus and Pomacentrus are definitely suitable for the beginner, and they will often live for years in the aquarium. They are not particularly demanding as regards their diet and will take all kinds of food, live and dead. Many species have bred in the aquarium. The eggs are laid in cichlid fashion within a small area on rocks, coral stumps and other firm objects on the bottom and are usually tended by both parents until the young hatch out. After this, brood protection ceases and the young have to look after themselves. This is now the difficult period, namely to find suitable foodstuffs for the tiny young which cannot take Artemia nauplii until they are 8–10 days old. The few successful rearings of these fishes have been achieved either by giving the fry marine plankton caught in temperate waters and taken to the aquarium, or by establishing a culture of the unicellular organism Euplotes in putrid sea water. After 8–10 days they can be given Artemia and finely sieved Cyclops. With the exception of the species of Chromis, most of the Pomacentridae are very territorial and often extremely aggressive towards members of their own species, genus and family. This should not, however, deter the aquar-

ist from keeping several individuals together with a view to eventually breeding them.

380. *Pomacentrus annulatus*
10 cm (3¾ in.). Indo-Pacific. A rarely imported species.

381. *Pomacentrus caeruleus*
10 cm (3¾ in.). Indo-Pacific. A hardy coral-reef fish that becomes very aggressive when adult.

382. *Abudefduf parasema*
[*Pomacentrus melanochir*]
8 cm (3 in.). Pacific Ocean. This fish is most attractive when young, and becomes very intolerant with age. The nomenclature of the fishes in the genus *Pomacentrus* is in a fairly confused state. There are, for example, several species which are mainly blue with yellow markings on the tail or hind part of the body and these can easily be confused. So, pending a thorough revision of the genus, even the specific names given here should be treated with a certain amount of reserve.

383. *Chromis caeruleus*
Blue Puller
13 cm (5 in.). Indo-Pacific and Red Sea. An elegant small shoaling fish which lives in the middle layers and feeds on plankton. In the aquarium it only thrives when kept in a small group. It quickly becomes accustomed to taking all kinds of small live and dead food. The eggs are laid on flat vertical surfaces and guarded mainly by the male. This species is very susceptible to bacterial infections of the skin.

384. *Chromis chromis*
12 cm (4¼ in.). Mediterranean Sea, along the coasts of southern Europe and northern Africa, extending into the eastern Atlantic Ocean. The young are a beautiful ultramarine blue. This species is well suited for an unheated marine tank, but it can also be kept in a coral-reef aquarium. Otherwise as for No. 383, but it is not so prone to shoal.

385. *Chromis dimidiatus*
9 cm (3½ in.). Indo-Pacific, where it is very common. This is a plankton-eater, and so it is often difficult to accustom it to substitute foods. In the aquarium it has a tendency to become aggressive and is very susceptible to skin infections.

386. *Abudefduf behni*
[*Abudefduf bitaeniatus*]
8 cm (3 in.). Indo-Pacific. A rarely imported fish. The species of the genus *Abudefduf* have similar aquarium requirements to those of *Pomacentrus*.

387. *Abudefduf oxyodon*
11 cm (4¼ in.). Indo-Pacific. A hardy species which lives in small shoals when young. The adults live solitarily or in pairs and in the aquarium they are very aggressive towards other members of their own species.

388. *Abudefduf saxatilis*
Sergeant Major
18 cm (7 in.). Indo-Pacific and tropical Atlantic. A shoaling species, in which the adults are often very territorial and aggressive.

389. *Dascyllus aruanus*
9 cm (3½ in.). Indo-Pacific and Red Sea. The species of this genus are among the hardiest of the coral-reef fishes. They are most attractive when young, and only then is it possible to keep several individuals together. When adult they can be extremely

aggressive, even towards other species. All the species mentioned here have spawned in the aquarium on several occasions, but very few have ever been successfully reared. According to F. de Graaf the female is smaller than the male and has a white marking on the forehead. The species of *Dascyllus* produce very loud sounds. In nature they sometimes live in among coral branches and, like the anemone-fishes, several species live in association with sea-anemones.

390. *Dascyllus melanurus*
7 cm (2¾ in.). Pacific Ocean.

391. *Dascyllus reticulatus*
7 cm (2¾ in.). Indo-Pacific.

392. *Dascyllus trimaculatus*
12 cm (4¾ in.). Indo-Pacific and Red Sea. A hardy species that is very commonly imported. It is most attractive when young, for the jet-black becomes more ash-grey with age. Like all the other species of *Dascyllus* the adults are often extremely aggressive towards other members of their own species. This fish has spawned on several occasions in aquarium tanks.

393. *Microspathodon chrysurus*
Yellowtail Damselfish
15 cm (6 in.). Tropical Atlantic and Caribbean Sea. The beautiful markings of the young stages become more blurred with age, and at the same time the adults become very aggressive towards other members of their own species and sometimes also towards other fishes.

Anemone-fishes
This is a group term used for the species in the genus *Amphiprion*.

They are also known as clownfishes. The term anemone-fishes refers to their close association with large tropical sea-anemones of the genera *Stoichactis, Discosoma* and *Radianthus*. Most fishes avoid sea-anemones, which have dangerous sting-cells in their tentacles, but the anemone-fishes have developed a form of behaviour which coats them with the mucus of the sea-anemone. They are then regarded as part of the sea-anemone, and the sting cells are not stimulated to fire. At one time it was thought that the anemone-fishes secreted a substance which blocked the firing of the anemone's sting cells but this theory has not stood up to close examination. Anemone-fishes that have been kept isolated from sea-anemones for a period of time are not able safely to touch one. This means that the fish must first become coated with anemone mucus before it can swim with impunity among the dangerous tentacles. Experiments with specimens of No. 395 which had been isolated from sea-anemones for months have shown that in every case this species can almost momentarily adapt itself to the anemone's tentacles. In nature certain anemone-fishes are associated with a given anemone species. An anemone-fish cannot therefore swim at will from one species of anemone to another without a period of acclimatisation.

The association is clearly advantageous for the anemone-fish which can seek shelter from the attacks of larger fishes among the anemone's tentacles. The advantage to the anemone is more doubtful, although from time to time it must benefit from scraps of food dropped among its tentacles by the fish.

In general, the anemone-fishes should be cared for in the same way as the other members of the family

Pomacentridae, but they are more delicate, and are more susceptible to the attacks of the parasitic protozoan *Oodinium*. Several species have bred in the aquarium, even for generations. Both male and female tend the eggs until they hatch. They usually lay their eggs in the vicinity of a sea-anemone, but this is not a prerequisite of successful breeding.

394. *Amphiprion biaculeatus*
[*Premnas biaculeatus*]
15 cm (6 in.). Philippines and the Indo-Australian Archipelago. Apart from its coloration this fish is distinguished from the other anemone-fishes by having one or two backward directed spines just below each eye. This is a somewhat difficult species which is aggressive towards its fellows.

395. *Amphiprion sandaracinos*
[*Amphiprion akallopisos*]
10 cm (3¾ in.). Indo-Pacific. This species is more tied to sea-anemones than most of the other anemone-fishes. In the Wilhelma Aquarium in Stuttgart it has been bred for several generations, using the one-celled organism *Euplotes* as food for the fry.

396. *Amphiprion allardi*
12 cm (4¾ in.). East coast of Africa from Mombasa to Dar-es-Salaam. This species was first described by W. Klausewitz in 1970 and named after the Belgian collector J. Allard of Mombasa.

397. *Amphiprion chrysopterus*
[*Amphiprion bicinctus*]
12 cm (4¾ in.). Indo-Pacific and Red Sea. A very variable species that is quite easy to keep. For aquarium

purposes it can be regarded as one of the hardier anemone-fishes.

398. *Amphiprion frenatus*
[*Amphiprion ephippium*]
15 cm (6 in.). Indo-Pacific. A variable species, in which the young stages usually have a white transverse band running from the back of the head down over each gill-cover. Some individuals develop a black marking on each flank as they grow older but in others this is lacking.

399. *Amphiprion ephippium*
[*Amphiprion frenatum*]
15 cm (6 in.). Philippines to Singapore. A very variable fish which resembles the preceding species.

400. *Amphiprion polymnus*
[*Amphiprion laticlavius*]
12 cm (4¾ in.). Pacific Ocean. A difficult species in the aquarium.

401. *Amphiprion ocellaris*
[*Amphiprion percula*]
10 cm (3¾ in.). Indo-Pacific, particularly in the eastern part. This is the best known and most commonly imported anemone-fish. It is not, however, so robust as many of the other *Amphiprion* species and is very susceptible to *Oodinium* infection. It has been bred a few times, and on at least one occasion the newly hatched fry were fed on plankton taken straight from the sea.

402. *Amphiprion perideraion*
8 cm (3 in.). Indo-Pacific. This is said to be a rather delicate species. It can be distinguished from No. 395 by the white band on the gill-cover.

403. *Amphiprion chrysopterus*
[*Amphiprion xanthurus*]
10 cm (3¾ in.). From East Africa to the Indo-Australian Archipelago. The

systematics of this very variable species is somewhat controversial. Thought to be a colour variety of No. 397.

Labridae
Wrasses

A large family with many tropical and subtropical species that are suitable for the aquarium. Their diet consists of a wide variety of live food, from the parasites removed from larger fishes by the Cleaner Wrasse to the corals crushed by other species. In the aquarium many of the wrasses are easy to keep and they are not so susceptible as other coral-reef fishes to the attacks of *Oodinium*. On the other hand, some species are sensitive to the metals, such as copper and zinc, used to treat diseases in other fishes. Many species spend the night lying on their side on the bottom, others (*Labroides*) produce special mucus 'sleeping-bags' or jelly-like bells in which they are protected from nocturnal predators, such as moray eels. Most of the Labridae quickly become accustomed to taking various substitute foods, both live and dead. There are no descriptions of successful breeding in the aquarium, although mating and spawning have been observed on several occasions. Many species spawn at random in the water (*Coris, Labroides, Thalassoma*); others practise brood protection. The eggs of the random spawners are very small and they rise to the surface. They hatch in about 24 hours and so far the tiny young have never been reared. It is characteristic of many wrasses that they pass through several colour phases at different periods of the life cycle. This has led to a certain amount of confusion in the nomenclature of the family.

404. *Bodianus axillaris*
[*Bodianus mesothorax*]

20 cm (7¾ in.). Indo-Pacific. The females and young are velvety-black with white markings. A hardy species which may live for years in the aquarium.

405. *Coris aygula*
[*Coris angulata*]

Up to 120 cm (47 in.). Indo-Pacific and Red Sea. The attractive juvenile pattern is replaced by a dirty grey or greenish pattern when the fish is *c.* 15–16 cm (*c.* 6 in.) long. A hardy, omnivorous species which with age may become somewhat aggressive towards its fellows.

406. *Coris gaimardi*
[*Coris formosa*]

40 cm (15¾ in.), but rarely more than 20 cm (7¾ in.) in the aquarium. Indo-Pacific. The illustration shows three colour stages of this fish. See also No. 407.

A very attractive and hardy fish which prefers a diet of small live crustaceans or worms. Like other wrasses, this species likes to be able to bury itself in a fine-grained substrate. These fish bury themselves at the start of the evening, punctually and independent of whether the lighting is turned off. They also bury themselves when frightened.

407. *Coris gaimardi*
[*Coris gaimard*]

40 cm (15¾ in.). Indo-Pacific. This is a colour stage of No. 406.

408. *Corisjulis*
Rainbow Wrasse

20 cm (7¾ in.). Mediterranean and eastern Atlantic. As in certain other wrasses, Rainbow Wrasses start life as females with a more brownish-grey pattern, a form once known as

Coris giofredi. In time male fish develop from these female phases, and they have the pattern shown in the illustration. The change of sex from female to male does not always take place at the same time as the change from the 'giofredi pattern' to the 'julis pattern'. It is therefore possible to find both 'giofredi males' and 'julis females', depending upon whether the sex change has taken place before or after the colour change. This is a hardy fish, but only suitable for a large, unheated Mediterranean tank. The young act as cleaners (see No. 412).

409. *Hemigymnus melapterus*
Up to 40 cm (15¾ in.). Indo-Pacific. An excellent aquarium fish when young. Unlike the *Coris* species this fish does not spend the night buried in the substrate, but in among coral branches or in cavities in the rockwork.

410. *Halichoeres hortulanus*
   [*Halichoeres centriquadrus*]
Up to 30 cm (11¾ in.). Indo-Pacific. An omnivorous fish which becomes very aggressive towards members of its own species when it is fully adult.

411. *Halichoeres marginatus*
Up to 30 cm (11¾ in.). Indo-Pacific. As for No. 410.

412. *Labroides dimidiatus*
   Cleaner Wrasse
10 cm (3¾ in.). Indo-Pacific. In the wild this and other species of *Labroides* feed mainly by removing parasites and scraps of skin from the skin and mouth cavity of larger fishes. They have a special way of approaching their 'client', with an undulatory swimming movement. This behaviour pattern inhibits any aggressive behaviour on the part of the client which remains in a fixed position in the water, effectively telling the wrasse that it is ready to be cleaned. Investigations on Cleaner Wrasses in the wild have shown that all the individuals are at first females, but when an individual succeeds in occupying a territory it develops into a male, its genital organs having both male and female cells. In a group of 6–8 fish only one is a male, the remainder being females or juveniles. If the dominant male dies, its place is taken over by the strongest female, which then becomes a male and mates with the females of the group. Cleaner Wrasses spend the night in among coral branches or in rock crevices lying in a bag of mucus which is formed as night falls and can be seen in the morning as a floating slough in the water.

In the aquarium Cleaner Wrasses may live for years, provided they are given at the start a sufficient amount of fine food, such as *Cyclops* and raw cod's roe. Many of them sicken and die if they are not fed properly. Large individuals are very aggressive towards one another.

413. *Pseudocheilinus hexataenia*
Up to 10 cm (3¾ in.), but rarely more than 6 cm (2¼ in.) in the aquarium. Indo-Pacific. An attractive fish which should not be kept with larger species. It quickly becomes accustomed to taking all kinds of live food. Several specimens can be kept together.

414. *Thalassoma bifasciatum*
   Bluehead
15 cm (6 in.). Caribbean Sea. The young, which are yellow, live in groups and act as cleaner-fish. When adult they make an attractive and very hardy aquarium fish. Blueheaded individuals are always male. This is a voracious fish which quickly

learns to take a wide variety of live food.

415. *Thalassoma lunare*
Green Wrasse
Up to 25 cm (9¾ in.). Indo-Pacific and Red Sea. A very voracious fish which should not be kept together with smaller species. There are several colour phases. At spawning time the male becomes pale sky-blue all over and chases the female very vigorously. Mating takes place just below the surface, the female laying some hundreds of small eggs which rise up to the surface. Spawning can extend over a period of several weeks in the course of which a female may produce hundreds of thousands of eggs. The young are very small and they have never been successfully reared in the aquarium. With age the males develop a large lyre-shaped caudal fin.

Acanthuridae
Surgeonfishes
A family of relatively large, often very brightly coloured fishes, which live in shoals in and near coral reefs, where they feed on vegetable matter. Spawning takes place at dusk, when a pair will separate off from the shoal and swim up below the surface, where the eggs are laid. After this the pair rejoins the shoal. The larvae have very long dorsal, anal and ventral fin rays. On each side of the base of the tail there is a scalpel-like spine which can be raised, hence the popular name. When a fish swims past an adversary with these spines erected it can cause serious injury. Care should be taken when catching up these fishes, as wounds caused by the spines can become infected, but no venom is involved.

On account of their size and specialised feeding habits surgeon fishes are not suitable for small private aquaria. In any case only small specimens should be kept, and then only in a large tank holding 400–500 litres (105½–132 U.S. gals).

416. *Acanthurus glaucopareius*
17 cm (6¾ in.). Philippines and neighbouring areas. A relatively hardy species in the aquarium.

417. *Acanthurus leucosternon*
30 cm (11¾ in.). Indian Ocean. A very attractive species but quite unsuitable for a private aquarium, as it needs large quantities of plant food.

418. *Acanthurus lineatus*
18 cm (7 in.). Indo-Pacific. Only young specimens are suitable for the private aquarium. Adults are very difficult to acclimatise.

419. *Paracanthurus hepatus*
[*Paracanthurus teuthis*]
30 cm (11¾ in.). Indo-Pacific. Only young specimens should be kept. The adults are usually difficult to acclimatise.

420. *Acanthurus achilles*
25 cm (9¾ in.). Hawaii and neighbouring areas. As in the case of the other surgeonfishes acclimatising this fish to the usual foods may be very difficult.

421. *Zebrasoma veliferum*
Up to 40 cm (15¾ in.). Indo-Pacific and Red Sea. This is probably the best surgeonfish for the aquarium. Young specimens are not difficult to acclimatise. When showing aggression they raise the large sail-like dorsal and anal fins. This is a very aggressive species which often lives for years in the aquarium.

422. *Zebrasoma xanthurum*
Up to 40 cm (15¾ in.). Indo-Pacific and Red-Sea. In specimens from the

Red Sea there is more blue on the body.

Scaridae
Parrotfishes
A large tropical family, the systematics of which are somewhat confused. They have a characteristic beak-like dentition, with which they can bite off and crush the corals that form an important part of their diet. Spawning takes place as described under *Thalassoma lunare*, No. 415. These are rather difficult fishes to acclimatise.

423. *Scarus frenatus*
    [*Scarus species*]
    Scarus sexvittatus
30 cm (11¾ in.). Indo-Pacific. The specimen illustrated is a male. Females and juveniles have a reddish ground colour. Not suitable for the private aquarium.

Balistidae
Triggerfishes
A large family of mainly tropical fishes with disproportionately large heads and powerful crushing teeth. The first dorsal fin ray is modified to form a powerful spine, which can be erected and locked into position by the second ray. In this way the fish can wedge itself fast in a rock crevice or in among blocks of coral.

Triggerfishes feed on shell-bearing molluscs and crustaceans which are crushed with the powerful jaws. In the aquarium they usually do quite well, but they should never be kept together with smaller fishes, as they are very voracious. They quickly become accustomed to taking all kinds of animal food, such as molluscs, fish flesh, prawns and so on. A few species have bred in captivity. Spawning takes place above a depression in the substrate.

424. *Balistapus undulatus*
30 cm (11¾ in.). Indo-Pacific. A very voracious species which when adult can only be kept in a large tank on its own.

425. *Balistoides niger*
    [*Balistoides conspicillum*]
Up to 50 cm (19½ in.). Indo-Pacific. This is a very popular fish which like No. 424 can be kept in a large tank. It is regarded as being more difficult to acclimatise, but once this has been done it is fairly hardy.

426. *Sufflamen chrysoptera*
    [*Hemibalistes chrysopterus*]
30 cm (11¾ in.). Indo-Pacific. An aggressive species that should be kept as described under the family.

427. *Melichthys vidua*
25 cm (9¾ in.). Indo-Pacific. Seldom imported. For care, see the family description.

428. *Rhinecanthus aculeatus*
    Picasso Fish
30 cm (11¾ in.). Indo-Pacific and the west coast of Africa. Small specimens are suitable for the aquarium, and usually do well. When large they become very voracious and may attack other fishes in the tank.

Monacanthidae
Filefishes
A family closely related to the triggerfishes. The front dorsal fin consists of two rays which are modified to form a locking mechanism, as in the triggerfishes. The ventral fins are each reduced to a single ray. Most of the species are peaceful, shoaling fishes. Many feed in nature on coral polyps, algae and a variety of small food, and having

such a specialised diet they may be difficult to acclimatise.

429. *Chaetoderma pencilligera*
 [*Monacanthus spinosissimus*]
18 cm (7 in.). Indo-Pacific. One of the easiest filefishes to keep.

430. *Oxymonacanthus longirostris*
10 cm (3¾ in.). Indo-Pacific. A typical shoaling species that feeds on corals and swims around with head down. It is usually very difficult to acclimatise to aquarium food. It will only thrive when kept in a small group. Single individuals invariably sicken.

Ostraciontidae
Boxfishes

These fishes have a characteristic box-like bony armour, with openings for the mouth, eyes, gills and fins; ventral fins are lacking. They are poor swimmers and move by the undulatory movements of the dorsal and anal fins, using the tail as a rudder. On account of their small mouth they require small food, which must at first be live. They are difficult to acclimatise, and when they die or are frightened they may release into the water a substance which is lethal to other fishes. The thin skin is very susceptible to infections. In general, the boxfishes can only be recommended for experienced aquarists.

431. *Lactoria cornuta*
50 cm (19½ in.). Indo-Pacific. Not really suitable for the aquarium.

432. *Ostracion meleagris*
 [*Ostracion lentiginosum*]
 Blue Boxfish
20 cm (7¾ in.). Indo-Pacific. The illustration shows a male. Like other boxfishes this species is difficult to acclimatise.

Opisthognathidae
Jawfishes

A small family with species found on sandy or gravelly bottoms, in which they dig vertical tunnels up to *c*. 30 cm (11¾ in.) in length. The mouth of the tunnel is usually strengthened by snail or bivalve shells. At night the fish retreats into its tunnel and closes the mouth with a shell or similar object. During the day it remains in the mouth of the tunnel and watches out for food. All the known species are mouth-brooders, but the young have not yet been reared in the aquarium.

433. *Opisthognathus aurifrons*
 Yellowhead Jawfish
12 cm (4¾ in.). Caribbean Sea. A species well suited to a small single-species tank. The substrate should be a mixture of various sizes of shells and coral fragments. They can be fed on small live and dead animal food.

Blenniidae
Blennies

A large family with representatives in all the seas of the world. Almost all the species occur in shallow waters near the coasts, where they live in rock crevices or holes. Some of the species in the genus *Blennius* can tolerate large fluctuations in salinity and temperature, such as occur in small intertidal rock pools, and can also withstand a considerable amount of organic pollution in the water.

434. *Aspidontus taeniatus*
 Sabre-toothed Blenny
10 cm (3¾ in.). Indo-Pacific. A fish that is strikingly similar to *Labroides dimidiatus* (No. 412) and yet belongs to a completely different family. On closer examination the two species can be distinguished from one

another by the mouth. In *Aspidontus taeniatus* this faces downwards and has long teeth, whereas in *Labroides dimidiatus* the mouth is terminal and the teeth are not visible. In *Aspidontus taeniatus* the dorsal fin starts farther forward than shown in its model, and the ventral fins are small and thin and positioned under the throat, whereas in *Labroides dimidiatus* the ventrals are larger and farther back on the underside of the body. The two fishes swim in the same way, but *Aspidontus taeniatus* has more body twisting.

This false cleaner lives in holes and empty worm tubes from which it sallies forth at great speed, and under false colours, nips off a piece of fin or flesh from a larger fish, which takes it for a true Cleaner Wrasse. In the aquarium this species should be kept by itself and fed on pieces of meat, mosquito larvae and similar animal food. It is not easy to keep and seldom lives long in captivity.

435. *Blennius nigriceps*
5 cm (2 in.). Mediterranean Sea. This little blenny lives on rocky coasts in depth of 4–6 feet, where it hides in holes and crevices. Like other *Blennius* species it is very voracious, so feeding presents no problems. It is sensitive to the presence of copper in the water.

436. *Blennius pavo*
12 cm (4¾ in.). Mediterranean Sea, where it is very common in harbours, bays and along the breakwaters in very shallow water. The males develop comb-like outgrowths on the head and indulge in violent territorial fights. This is an omnivorous species that is not difficult to keep in the aquarium, provided it is given plenty of hiding places, such as drainpipes or inverted flowerpots. The male guards the eggs.

437. *Blennius sphinx*
    Sphinx Blenny
8 cm (3 in.). Mediterranean Sea, in shallow water along rocky coasts, where it lives right in the surf zone. The male is more brightly coloured than the female and has larger fins and long outgrowths on the forehead. A hardy species, but it has a tendency to eat too much, so it should be fed in moderation.

438. *Ecsenius pulcher*
10 cm (3¾ in.). Indo-Pacific. The male is larger than the female and has longer anal fin rays. It should be kept as a pair or in a group of one male and several females, as the males are very aggressive towards one another. It is not a difficult fish, but is best kept in a separate tank without other species but with plenty of hiding-places. Although omnivorous it should always have access to a good supply of algal food. This species is sometimes incorrectly placed in a separate family known as the Clinidae.

Gobiidae
Gobies
This is a very large family with species in all seas, and a few in fresh waters. They lack a lateral line and the ventral fins are modified to form a sucker. With a few exceptions they are typical bottom-living species, and heavier than water. There are two dorsal fins, and the large pectoral fins are used in swimming. Most of the gobies are omnivorous and very voracious, hardy aquarium fishes. Many species have spawned in captivity, and they all protect the brood.

439. *Gobiodon citrinus*
    [*Gobiodon citrinellus*]
4 cm (1½ in.). Indo-Pacific and Red Sea. This goby is best kept in a small

tank on its own or in a tank with marine invertebrates. An omnivorous but very shy species which often seeks shelter in the crowns of tube-dwelling bristle-worms.

440. *Gobiosoma oceanops*
[*Elacatinus oceanops*]
Neon Goby
6 cm (2¼ in.). West Indies to southern Florida. On account of its small size this goby should not be kept with large species, but does best in a tank with invertebrates. It can be fed on small live food, such as *Artemia*, *Cyclops* or small scraps of fish flesh or roe. In nature it behaves as a cleaner fish (note how similar it is in appearance to *Labroides*). Neon Gobies have spawned several times in the tanks of U.S. aquarists. The eggs are laid in holes and guarded by both parents which are said to continue tending the young fish. They are very sensitive to *Oodinium* and to the copper used to treat this disease.

441. *Ptereleotris tricolor*
14 cm (5½ in.). Indo-Pacific. Unlike most of the other gobies this is a free-swimming fish which lives in pairs or small shoals in the vicinity of coral reefs. It is rather shy but fairly hardy in the aquarium.

Ephippidae U.S.A.
Platacidae Britain
Batfishes
A small family related to the Chaetodontidae. They live in coastal waters, the young and juveniles often in brackish water near estuaries. The young can assume remarkable positions, which make them look like withered leaves drifting in the stream. The dorsal, anal and ventral fins are enormously elongated, particularly in the young. With increasing age

they become more like a discus fish in shape. They often suffer fatal injuries during transport, but young undamaged specimens do well in the aquarium and have a ravenous appetite. Growth is rapid and indeed batfishes have a tendency to outgrow their tank. When adult they are only suitable for a public aquarium. They are very aggressive and should either be kept singly or in a group of 4–5, all of the same size. They are very susceptible to skin and fin infections which are difficult to cure. All the species occur in the Indo-Pacific region.

442. *Platax orbicularis*
50 cm (19½ in.). The coloration varies from pale brown to almost black. Some individuals develop pale markings on the flanks. This is the most commonly imported form.

443. *Platax pinnatus*
40 cm (15¾ in.). Possibly the most attractive species. The attractive red edging of the young disappears with age.

444. *Platax teira*
50 cm (19½ in.). In young specimens of this species the distance between the tips of the dorsal and anal fins is up to three times as great as the body length.

Scorpaenidae
Scorpionfishes
A large and widely distributed family in which some species live in sheltered positions. Many show protective coloration and develop outgrowths of skin which enhance their camouflage. The head and mouth are usually large and many species have poisonous spines on the gill covers, so extreme care must be taken when

handling them; this applies particularly to the dragonfishes. Wounds caused by these spines are very painful and may prove fatal to particularly sensitive persons. In every case the tank should be positioned and covered in such a way that strangers, and in particular children, cannot reach the fish.

445. *Dendrochirus brachypterus*
15 cm (6 in.). Indo-Pacific. This species often remains hidden during the day. It can be fed at first on live fish, such as guppies, but some individuals will become accustomed to taking dead animal food.

446. *Pterois radiata*
20 cm (7¾ in.). Indo-Pacific and Red Sea. It may be difficult to acclimatise this fish to take dead food.

447. *Pterois volitans*
Dragonfish or Turkeyfish
35 cm (13¾ in.). Indo-Pacific. Most beautiful as young specimens, when the pectoral and dorsal fin rays are at their longest in relation to the body. It usually acclimatises very quickly to dead food, and being voracious it will then grow rapidly. It should only be kept with fishes of its own size, as smaller ones are regarded as prey. Dragonfishes probably breed near to estuaries, as young specimens are often found in brackish waters close to the coast.

Callionymidae
Dragonets
A small family with only 6 genera and about 22 species described, although there are certain to be more species yet to be discovered in the tropics.

448. *Synchiropus splendidus*
7 cm (2¾ in.). Philippines and neighbouring areas, in the vicinity of the coasts. Sex difference: in the male the foremost rays of the first dorsal fin are much elongated. This species should only be kept in a separate tank, without other fishes. It is very difficult to get it to take the usual aquarium foods, and it only eats very little at a time. The main problem is to find the right type of food, but attempts should be made with *Tubifex*, small crustaceans (both marine and freshwater), mosquito and midge larvae, and *Artemia*.

Plotosidae

449. *Plotosus lineatus*
Up to 70 cm (27½ in.). Indo-Pacific. This fish belongs to a mainly marine family of catfishes. When young it lives in dense shoals in shallow water. In captivity it will thrive best if kept in a group of 6–8 individuals. This is a very voracious species which is not really suitable for a private aquarium. They start to become sexually mature when 15–30 cm (6–12 in.) long. The females are then very stout and often die because they are unable to spawn. Old specimens are sometimes very aggressive.

Centriscidae
A small family of very odd-looking fishes. They normally swim with the head down, searching for food animals on the bottom or in among the spines of sea-urchins (*Diadema*), with which they have a form of symbiotic association. They should be kept in a tank on their own and fed as frequently as possible on small live food, such as *Cyclops*, small *Mysis*, *Daphnia*, mosquito larvae or newly born guppies until they become accustomed to accepting dead food. The conditions for breeding are unknown.

450. *Aeoliscus strigatus*
Shrimpfish
12 cm (4¾ in.). Indo-Pacific. For care, see the family description.

Syngnathidae
Sea-horses and Pipefishes
A large family of rather odd-looking fishes which live in areas of coastal seaweed. Sea-horses have a prehensile tail with which they hold on to the vegetation, while the long, slender body of the pipefishes enables them to curl round vegetation. All the species have a characteristic form of brood protection. During pairing the female lays her eggs and transfers them to a brood pouch or groove on the belly of the male. There the eggs develop into miniature replicas of the parents, and then leave the brood pouch. In the aquarium sea-horses and pipefishes will only thrive if they can be given a sufficient amount of the correct type of live food. Large specimens will do well on *Mysis*, and some individuals will become accustomed to taking mosquito larvae or young guppies. Sea-horses do not belong in a coral-reef aquarium, but should be given a tank on their own with a bottom filter and dead horny corals to which they can cling. They are sensitive to sudden changes in the amount of dissolved gas in the sea water; if this increases too much air bubbles will appear below the skin and in the blood, and death may ensue.

451. *Dunckerocampus caulleryi*
  [*Dunckerocampus
  dactyliophorus*]
16 cm (6¼ in.). Philippines and the Indo-Australian Archipelago. This attractive species should be kept in water with a specific gravity of 1·025

and at a temperature of 25–27°C (77–81°F). It can be fed on *Artemia* and other small crustaceans.

452. *Hippocampus guttulatus*
18 cm (7 in.). Eastern Atlantic and Mediterranean. To be kept in unheated water (specific gravity 1·025–1·026) and without other fishes. The male carries the developing eggs for about 6 weeks. The young, of which there may be up to 300, are difficult to rear as they do not do well on *Artemia* nauplii.

453. *Hippocampus hudsonius*
20 cm (7¾ in.). Western tropical Atlantic. A very variable species, to be kept in water with a specific gravity of 1·024–1·026 at a temperature of 22–26°C (72–79°F). It requires large amounts of food but can be acclimatised to take small guppies.

454. *Hippocampus kuda*
  Golden Sea-horse
15 cm (6 in.). Indo-Pacific. The coloration varies from dark brown to lemon-yellow. Temperature of the water 25–27°C (77–81°F).

455. *Hippocampus zosterae*
  Dwarf Sea-horse
5 cm (2 in.). West Indies. This very small sea-horse must be kept in a tank on its own and treated on the lines given in the family description. It can be fed on newly hatched *Artemia* and it is said that these can also be given to the young, which have been reared in the United States. The natural longevity is only about one year. The male carries the developing eggs for 10–14 days, and the young become sexually mature after a few months. Temperature: 18–22°C (64–72°F); specific gravity: 1·020–1·024.

REPRODUCTIVE METHODS

The last three colour plates show some typical methods of reproduction in the fishes described in this book. The number alongside each silhouette refers to a species that shows the relevant mode of reproduction. In the case of the red-brown silhouettes the male and/or female signs denote whether one or both sexes are responsible for brood protection. The ochre-coloured silhouettes (Nos. 56, 60, 98, 167, 320, 349 and 415) show egg-laying by females of species which do not protect their brood. The two dark brown silhouettes (Nos. 230 and 232) show live-bearing fishes. Nos. 16–330 are all freshwater species, Nos. 389–454 are from sea water.

Freshwater Fishes
A. Numerous small eggs are laid in the vicinity of or in among plants, to which most of them adhere.
B. Usually numerous eggs, which are laid at random in the water and then sink to the bottom.
C. Eggs containing oil, which are laid at random in the water and then rise to the surface.
D. Eggs, usually only a few, laid in the substrate.
E. Eggs laid on leaves above the water.
F. Eggs laid on submerged leaves.
G. Eggs laid in a bubble-nest at the surface (Nos. 314 and 325) or among plant stems below the surface (No. 330).
H. Three methods of egg-laying in cichlids which do not hide their eggs, namely on leaves, rocks or the bottom respectively.
I. Examples of cichlids which lay their eggs hidden in rock crevices or under stones.
J. Eggs laid in shallow pits in the bottom, either uncovered (J1) or covered with sand or similar (J2).
K. Two mouth-brooding species.
L. Two live-bearing species.

Marine Fishes
A. Eggs are laid near the surface and rise.
B. Eggs are laid at random in the water and sink to the bottom.
C. Mouth-brooding.
D. Eggs develop into young within a brood pouch on the male's belly.
E, F, G. Eggs laid on firm substrates.

BIBLIOGRAPHY

Allen, G. R., *The Anemonefishes: Their Classification and Biology*, TFH Publications, Neptune City, New Jersey, 1972.

Axelrod, H. R. and Schultz, L. P., *Handbook of Tropical Aquarium Fishes*, McGraw-Hill, New York and London, 1955.

Duijn, C. van, *Diseases of Fishes*, Iliffe Books, London, (new edn.) 1967.

Faulkner, D. and Atz, J. W., *Aquarium Fishes: Their Beauty, History and Care,* Viking Press, New York, 1971.

Fryer, G. and Iles, T. D., *The Cichlid Fishes of the Great Lakes of Africa*, Oliver & Boyd, Edinburgh and TFH Publications, Neptune City, New Jersey, 1972.

Jackman, L. A. J., *Marine Aquaria*, David & Charles, Newton Abbot and London, 1968.

Knowles, F. G. W., *Freshwater and Saltwater Aquaria*, Harrap & Co., London, 1953.

Lagler, K. F., Bardach, J. E. and Miller, R. R., *Ichthyology, the Study of Fishes*, John Wiley & Sons, New York and London, 1962.

McInerny, D. and Gerard, G., *All About Tropical Fish*, Harrap & Co., London and Macmillan Publishing Co. Inc., New York, 1958, 1967.

Marshall, N. B., *The Life of Fishes*, Weidenfeld & Nicolson, London, 1965 and Universe Books, New York, 1966.

Marshall, T. C., *Fishes of the Great Barrier Reef and Coastal Waters of Queensland*, Angus & Robertson, Sydney, 1964.

Norman, J. R. and Greenwood, P. H., *A History of Fishes*, Benn, London, 1963.

Randall, J. E., *Caribbean Reef Fishes*, TFH Publications, Neptune City, New Jersey, 1968.

Spotte, S., *Marine Aquarium Keeping*, John Wiley & Sons, New York, 1973.

Sterba, G., *Freshwater Fishes of the World*, Vista Books, London, 1962.

Sterba, G., *Aquarium Care*, Studio Vista, London, 1967.

PERIODICALS

The Aquarist and Pondkeeper, Buckley Press, London and Brentford, England.

The Aquarium, Pet Books Inc., Maywood, New Jersey.

Tropical Fish Hobbyist, TFH Publications, Neptune City, New Jersey and Reigate, England.

INDEX OF LATIN NAMES

(Numbers refer both to colour plates and to descriptive notes.)

239

INDEX OF ENGLISH NAMES

(Numbers refer both to colour plates and to descriptive notes.)